BORN IN SLAVERY

*The Story of Methodism in Anguilla
and its influence in the Caribbean*

BORN IN SLAVERY

*The Story of Methodism in Anguilla
and its influence in the Caribbean*

Edited by
Wilbert Forker

DUNEDIN ACADEMIC PRESS
EDINBURGH

Published by
Dunedin Academic Press Ltd
Hudson House
8 Albany Street
Edinburgh EH1 3QB
Scotland

ISBN 1 903765 13 7

British Library Cataloguing in Publication Data
A catalogue record for this book is available from the British Library

Typeset by Patty Rennie Production, Portsoy
Printed in Great Britain by Cromwell Press

Contents

Thanks

Our thanks are due to the Methodist Conference of the Caribbean and the Americas for the use of the Conference Hymn written by The Reverend Hugh B Sherlock and to the British Methodist Conference for the use of hymns from the Methodist Hymn Book.

The photograph of the Wilberforce memorial in Westminster Abbey is used by courtesy of the Dean and Chapter of Westminster.

A special thank you to Mrs Helen Peabody for her editorial contribution and her skills in preparing the manuscript for publication.

And to the Christian Literature Trust for financing the publication.

Foreword

Methodism in Anguilla and the Caribbean was born in slavery.

The slaves were of different hues, mostly brought from the disease-ridden West African countries, while others were brought in densely overcrowded wooden sloops from the plantation States of Georgia, the Carolinas and their direct neighbours to an uncertain future in the British controlled islands of the Caribbean.

By 1760 slaves were being set free in Antigua after Nathaniel Gilbert, an island landlord, politician and slave owner, was redeemed during a visit to London where he invited John Wesley to preach at his home. This was some 80 years before emancipation became law. It was from Antigua and the sister islands that the freed slaves, enriched by salvation, freedom and liberty, sailed through this pearl-strung group of sun-kissed islands with their revolutionary message of salvation and justice, encountering strong and at times violent opposition from a scared English minority who rightly saw these preachers as a severe threat to their comfortable life-style.

Over the next several years some colonial governors attempted the 'divide and rule' method of governing as a way of keeping the lid on the spiritual revolution that was taking shape in their midst. But that was proved to be a short-lived, ill-thought, non-workable method of governing and enabled the undaunted freed slaves to establish meeting places on the islands as centres for worship and song. This was to pave the way for schools as a source of learning and awareness building and which, when coupled with the message of the redeeming love and social justice, was dynamite in the Caribbean.

The story that follows has been written by the sons of those freed slaves and combined represents some 250 years of witness and service in the islands of the Caribbean; in Belize in Central America and Guyana on the South American mainland. Some repetition is necessary to enable each chapter tell its own story.

Their story is unique. From the small most northerly Leeward island of Anguilla a constant stream of men and women have offered themselves as the successors of their born in slavery forefathers. The thoroughness of their theological education and their training for ministry in these island communities is seen in their own success. The same applies to the laity who from this small 35 square mile island have migrated to other islands mostly for professional and economic reasons, and who have established worship and witness centres in their adopted islands.

What commenced as Methodism sailing to the slave and indentured island of Anguilla and to the other Caribbean gems, is today an island proud of its witness and influence in the Caribbean Church, State and society and its people are determined to continue not just a tradition but a positive response to the Divine call, "Follow me . . ."

Wilbert Forker
Editor
1 May 2003

TO THE MEMORY OF
WILLIAM WILBERFORCE
(BORN IN HULL AUGUST 24th 1759,
DIED IN LONDON JULY 29th 1833.)
FOR NEARLY HALF A CENTURY A MEMBER OF THE HOUSE OF COMMONS
AND, FOR SIX PARLIAMENTS DURING THAT PERIOD,
ONE OF THE TWO REPRESENTATIVES FOR YORKSHIRE.
IN AN AGE AND COUNTRY FERTILE IN GREAT AND GOOD MEN,
HE WAS AMONG THE FOREMOST OF THOSE WHO FIXED THE CHARACTER OF THEIR TIMES
BECAUSE TO HIGH AND VARIOUS TALENTS,
TO WARM BENEVOLENCE, AND TO UNIVERSAL CANDOUR,
HE ADDED THE ABIDING ELOQUENCE OF A CHRISTIAN LIFE.
EMINENT AS HE WAS IN EVERY DEPARTMENT OF PUBLIC LABOUR,
AND A LEADER IN EVERY WORK OF CHARITY,
WHETHER TO RELIEVE THE TEMPORAL OR THE SPIRITUAL WANTS OF HIS FELLOW MEN
HIS NAME WILL EVER BE SPECIALLY IDENTIFIED
WITH THOSE EXERTIONS
WHICH BY THE BLESSING OF GOD, REMOVED FROM ENGLAND
THE GUILT OF THE AFRICAN SLAVE TRADE,
AND PREPARED THE WAY FOR THE ABOLITION OF SLAVERY
IN EVERY COLONY OF THE EMPIRE:
IN THE PROSECUTION OF THESE OBJECTS,
HE RELIED, NOT IN VAIN, ON GOD;
BUT IN THE PROGRESS, HE WAS CALLED TO ENDURE
GREAT OBLOQUY AND GREAT OPPOSITION:
HE OUTLIVED, HOWEVER, ALL ENMITY;
AND, IN THE EVENING OF HIS DAYS,
WITHDREW FROM PUBLIC LIFE AND PUBLIC OBSERVATION
TO THE BOSOM OF HIS FAMILY.
YET HE DIED NOT UNNOTICED OR FORGOTTEN BY HIS COUNTRY:
THE PEERS AND COMMONS OF ENGLAND,
WITH THE LORD CHANCELLOR AND THE SPEAKER AT THEIR HEAD,
IN SOLEMN PROCESSION FROM THEIR RESPECTIVE HOUSES,
CARRIED HIM TO HIS FITTING PLACE
AMONG THE MIGHTY DEAD AROUND,
HERE TO REPOSE:
TILL, THROUGH THE MERITS OF JESUS CHRIST,
HIS ONLY REDEEMER AND SAVIOUR,
(WHOM, IN HIS LIFE AND IN HIS WRITINGS HE HAD DESIRED TO GLORIFY,)
HE SHALL RISE IN THE RESURRECTION OF THE JUST.

While the Emancipation Bill was being passed in the British Parliament, Wilberforce lay on his deathbed. The frail little man had long been the icon of the British people. When he heard that the Emancipation Bill was to be passed, he exclaimed in triumph, "Thank God that I should have lived to witness a day in which England is willing to give twenty millions sterling for the abolition of slavery!" Four days later, he died.

Chapter 1

Methodism Sails to the Caribbean

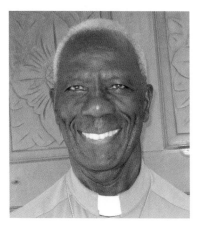

The Reverend Franklin A Roberts*

Whatever may be the expectation of those who take note of the above title, it is most important to make an early disclosure that the main purpose of writing this book is to document a History of Methodism in Anguilla.

It is anticipated that the majority of readers will not be from Anguilla or even the Caribbean! To some of our readers, Anguilla may well be as unknown today as it was to a host of Jamaicans, when two of us – Rev John A Gumbs and myself – made our way to Caenwood Theological College in Jamaica for theological training in 1947. Even fellow-students from Jamaica numbered among "The Holy Seven", knew nothing about Anguilla's existence! Every opportunity was deliberately taken to penetrate Church and Society and – as was said by observers – "put Anguilla on the map!" It goes without saying how very interesting it was for some of us who later visited Britain and elsewhere to proudly reveal that we hail from Anguilla, and then proceed to lighten their darkness!

---

* See biographical note, page 66.

Despite the passing of years, the political upheaval and "The Revolution" in Anguilla in 1967 that gave prominence to the island, it is still appropriate to briefly present some historical details with regard to the island.

Local historians in Anguilla are not slow to side with those who date the discovery of Caribbean islands long before the arrival of Christopher Columbus in 1492. One of Anguilla's sons, Colville Petty – author, historian and curator of Heritage Collection Museum – has something to say about this 35 square mile island situated 18.2 degrees North Latitude and 63 degrees West Longitude, with a population of approximately 11,000. Our local historian writes: "Anguilla, once a lush island with a dense rain forest, was discovered some 4,000 years ago by an Arawak speaking Amerindian people who called it 'Malliouhana'".

Just as the peaceful Arawaks were wiped out in other Caribbean islands, the same holds good in regard to Anguilla. When the English settlers came to Anguilla in 1650, there were no Arawaks on the island.

Anguilla's social and political history has been one of struggle and conflict. The story will long be told of the sterling qualities of an extraordinary people who passed through the fire of slavery, social deprivation, and the imposition of unbearable political bonds. Anguilla today, is a good and peaceful island in which to live. Social and economic conditions have improved considerably. Like the few remaining British Dependent Territories, Anguilla is in dialogue with "Mother England" in regard to Constitutional affairs affecting the welfare of its people.

No credible historian can write on the topic "Methodism Sails to the Caribbean" without acknowledging that it all started in the Caribbean island of Antigua. What a thrilling story! We are brought face to face with the God who "moves in a mysterious way His wonders to perform". The prominent place of laypersons in bringing Methodist congregations to birth and keeping alive the mission of God in very trying times, will long be recounted.

Let us take a brief look at a few details: The setting is in Antigua in the 1750's where the iniquitous system of slavery was "good business." Nathaniel Gilbert – Lawyer, Plantation Owner and Speaker of the Island House of Assembly – who John Wesley in his diary dated 29th November 1758 wrote of as "a gentleman lately come from Antigua" – was caught up in what Wesley himself described as "that execrable sum of all Villainy".

The God who "works His purpose out" led Nathaniel Gilbert as he convalesced from a recent illness to request his five-year-old daughter,

Mary, to fetch a recent publication from his library. Mary mistakenly carried him a forgotten pamphlet entitled "An Appeal to Men of Reason and Religion", sent to him by his brother, Francis. Nathaniel reluctantly read the book. So impressed was he, he decided to visit England and hear John Wesley preach. He took with him three of his slave women. A drawing-room meeting was arranged at Wandsworth in London. As a consequence of Wesley's preaching, Nathaniel and his slaves were converted to Christ. This Service had far-reaching results, for it enabled Methodism to 'Sail to the Caribbean'.

Returning to Antigua, Nathaniel Gilbert whose "heart was full of Christ", not only gathered his family and friends, but his slaves as well, and shared with them the Good News of the Gospel. Devoted slave women, and John Baxter – the English shipwright and Methodist Local Preacher – who arrived in Antigua in 1778 to work at the dockyard in English Harbour, carried on this "great work" begun in 1760. Baxter later resigned from his occupation, to secure more time for preaching the Gospel.

Dr Thomas Coke, whom John Wesley set apart to superintend the mission in America and the Caribbean, was authorized to ordain Baxter as a minister at the Conference held in Baltimore in 1784. Returning to Antigua with the status of an Elder, Baxter continued to throw himself into the work, which was at this time growing by leaps and bounds. He rejoiced at the fulfilment of his prayer for ministerial help when Dr Coke together with William Warrener, William Hammett and John Clarke landed in St. John's on Christmas Morning 1786. The ship in which Coke and his companions travelled had set sail on 24 September bound for Nova Scotia, where Hammett and Clarke were stationed by the British Conference. The voyage was the occasion of danger, frustration and near disaster. At the end of it all, Coke felt that God was at work. He wrote: "All is as clear as if it were written with a sunbeam". After consulting Baxter, Coke tore up the Appointments made by Conference, and stationed John Clarke in St Vincent and William Hammett in St Kitts; leaving William Warrener with Baxter in Antigua. Coke then returned to England. He would be busier than ever with his appeals for "benevolent subscribers" for the work overseas, and to seek out other young men of good sense and great piety who would volunteer for service in the Caribbean.

As we focus attention on "Methodism Sails to the Caribbean", it is worthy of note that whereas in all, or most Territories of the Methodist Church in the Caribbean and the Americas (MCCA), Methodism was introduced by non-natives, it was altogether different in Anguilla. An Anguillian is documented as being responsible for the birth of

Methodism in his homeland. Anguillians have always been cognizant of the need – particularly as a Church – to be self-propagating and self-supporting. More will be said with respect to the impressive list of "Sons of the soil" who heard and responded to the call to propagate the faith. The story will be told of the faithfulness and commitment of humble laymen and women who over the years carried on the work, which had been started by the pioneer – John Hodge.

Though there is certainty in regard to the conversion of John Hodge – for as Jesus said: "by their fruits you shall know them" – there is uncertainty as to where exactly the miracle of grace took place. It is assumed that this "free coloured" man was converted to Christ and Methodism in either St Barths or St Eustatius. I am led to believe that it all happened in St Eustatius where he directly or indirectly came under the influence of Black Harry whose heart had been aflame for Christ.

There in his homeland, Mr Hodge in 1813 petitioned the Deputy Governor for permission to preach to the slaves who were many! At that time Anguilla was without any form of religious institution since the French invasion in 1796. Having been granted permission, John Hodge went about the task with great fervour and zeal. Much success attended him. When in 1817 the Deputy Governor received a request from the British Parliament seeking information on the social and moral conditions in several West Indian Territories, he did not hesitate to respond in glowing terms, highlighting the accomplishment of John Hodge:

> The unexpected introduction of religion took place in the year 1813 in which I received a letter from John Hodge, a free coloured man and native of the island, importuning my sanction for the establishment of it. Deeming it essential to the reformation of the slaves, who, before that period, were conducting themselves in habitual violation of the whole system of morality, and with a view to discipline them in their duty to God and man, I readily offered every encouragement to the petitioner, who proceeded to discharge his religious duties as a Local Preacher without the most trifling procrastination, until Class Meetings were established and leaders appointed to investigate them: which duties he still continues to discharge.

As we think of John Hodge – the pioneer of Methodism in Anguilla – we are furnished with yet another instance of the "God who uses the weak things of this world to confound the mighty". And like great Church Leaders such as St Augustine, we see in the life of John Hodge the triumph of the transforming grace of God. In a letter dated 11 July 1828, written to the Wesleyan Mission House in London by Rev Henry Britten – John Hodge's successor – testimony is given of wonders wrought through the changed life of this Anguillian, who like St Paul, gave up former delights for "the excellency of knowing God", and proclaiming Good News to his people:

> The Society in this island has evidently been raised by the mighty power of God. The people were altogether without religious instruction when the grace of God laid hold on the conscience of a young man of colour who had been a notorious sinner particularly addicted to the cruel and irrational sport of cockfighting. He gave up his sinful pleasures and companions and became a thoroughly changed character and soundly converted man. He immediately began to publish to his neighbours the great blessing he had found in religion. Some "mocked", others "believed the report", and a little Society was raised which flourished under his fostering care. During eight or ten years, he most indefatigably travelled the island watching over his flock, expounding and preaching Jesus to all. For eight years or upward, he had to labour industriously to provide for his family, while thus engaged in the work of the Lord: but during the last six years he has been entirely given up to the work; and in February last when going to his new Appointment, he left behind him a Society of about 500 persons. He was universally and very deservedly beloved by all parties.

Rev James Whitworth, who visited Anguilla from St Barths, the nearby French island, left on record the testimony of a resident proprietor who was formerly prejudiced against Methodism. The proprietor stated that since its coming "there has been an almost entire cessation of dancing, wakes and carousing among the slaves, in consequence of which they enjoy good health, and have scarcely any need of doctors". Grateful for this change of life on the part of his slaves, he gave a very handsome donation and the labour of his slaves towards the building of a local Methodist Church.

It is too soon to determine whether or not the words found in St Luke chapter four verse twenty-four: "Truly I tell you, no prophet is accepted in the prophet's homeland", are applicable to the present "Son of the Soil": now Superintendent Minister of the Anguilla Circuit. In regard to our pioneer, however, the validity of the saying may well be questioned.

When John Hodge returned to Anguilla in 1813, he started working on his own. By the year 1815 when Rev C Riley visited, John Hodge was head of 250 Methodists. On Riley's recommendation, John Hodge was officially appointed as Lay Agent, and in 1818 the Anguilla Circuit of 169 members appeared on the list of Stations of the British Methodist Conference. There was a promise that a Minister who would reside in Anguilla would be sent.

At the Antigua Synod in 1818, John Hodge was recommended as a Candidate for the itinerant ministry. After a probation period of four years, he was ordained and his name appears on the list of Stations for 1822 – the first black West Indian to be so honoured! The membership in Anguilla was now 220. John Hodge continued his ministry in Anguilla till 1827, and served a second term from 1832 to 1835. His passion to "kindle the flame" in nearby St Martin saw fulfilment. As early as 1817 he sailed across the channel and landed in Marigot on the French side of the small island. The success of his crowded meetings was interrupted, when the French Commandant, struck with alarm, expelled him and his supporters. John Hodge and his followers then crossed the border to the Dutch side of the island and established the mission there.

Unwillingness on the part of some itinerant ministers to be uprooted and move on to a new Circuit or District Conference is not new. Sometimes active support is received from members of the flock and even from External Organizations and high-ranking officials! This kind of outworking can be seen with respect to our pioneer. When our Church Authorities in London wanted to send John Hodge to work in Africa, two Ministers were chosen to interview him with a view to the appointment. Those who examined him had this to say: "Hodge ranks high as any coloured man in all the West Indies. He is company for the Governor and the Legislature. His person is comely, his manners graceful; his language rather neat than bombastic: his soul burns with holy fervour, and his will is greatly subdued and acting that of God – in short he is qualified for the work proposed in every particular".

It is said that Hodge made himself so indispensable in Anguilla that the proposed Appointment to Africa was never made. But did Hodge and his supporters really want him to leave and go to unknown Africa?

In what follows, we see the Lieutenant Governor of Anguilla in 1819 coming again to the rescue of John Hodge, and successfully thwarting the plan of the Church in regard to his Stationing. The Lt Governor wrote to the Wesleyan Missionary Society in London on the matter of John Hodge being discriminated against by his white colleagues at the District Meeting:

Permit me to call your attention to the seeming of prejudice, which prevailed among some of the Missionary Gentlemen, while in the island of Antigua against John Hodge who attended by their desire. Those Gentlemen, not only viewed themselves in superiority to him, and made it manifest that his colour sufficed for the evidence of their inattention to him (Except the Chairman – the Rev Gilgrass and Rev W White) but concluded on sending him to Saint Domingo for life. At first Hodge consented, but with this proviso, that one of the Missionaries would accompany him. This was objected, and in consequence he is directed to preach the Gospel under Rev Ranar who is appointed to the island of St Martin . . . such an occurrence has caused much grief and displeasure to the inhabitants of Anguilla.

Again the question is asked: Did the Servant of the Church want to leave Anguilla and go to Santo Domingo – the unknown? And were the Lt Governor and fellow-Anguillians who were given first-hand information desirous of releasing their popular and highly esteemed hero?

The successors of Rev John Hodge continued the process of sowing and nurturing the seed of the Gospel. Elsewhere in this book, reference will be made to the extension and erection of places of worship. The names of Revs Henry Britten, Jonathan Cadman, Matthew Banks and John Croft, will live on as the story of early Methodism is told. By the year 1832 the Church Roll showed a membership of 617. It was however most unfortunate that due to financial constraints there was no resident minister for the period 1837–1867. As a consequence, the membership rapidly decreased, until a great revival took place when Dirk Almair Schouten appeared on the scene – first as a Lay Agent, and then as an Ordained Minister. His ministry in Anguilla was unique. He served from 1867–1909. On transfer to the British Virgin Islands – altogether different from Anguilla – this worn-out soldier died within months. He had fought a good fight, and finished his work.

Nearly 250 years ago, Methodism sailed to the Caribbean. Those who came as servants of Christ and the Church, and whose hearts were set aflame, were all bearers of the 'Good News', at a time when exploitation, conflicts and slavery – with all its attendant evils – were the order of the day.

Comparison has been made between Don Christopher Columbus and Dr Thomas Coke – the Columbus of West Indian Methodism. Whereas the former who set sail from the little Spanish town of Palos came primarily to plunder and gain, the Columbus of West Indian Methodism came to give. From anchorage to anchorage, Don Christopher "chased this yellow will-o'-the-wisp – gold". Coke travelled from island to island with the greatest story to tell to the nations. To our poor benighted forebears, bruised and crushed by the iniquitous system of slavery, Dr Coke, John Hodge, Black Harry, the Gilberts, John Baxter, and the rest whose hearts God opened, boldly proclaimed tidings of great joy. They told of the glorious liberty of the children of God; "for if the Son shall set you free, you shall be free indeed".

What is the challenge to us today? From pulpit to pew we would do well to adopt the kind of resolve individually and collectively entered upon as a thankful people celebrated the opening of a new church in one of our Circuits. The June Quarterly Meeting in 1841 adopted this Resolution: "This Meeting individually and collectively pledges itself, in humble dependence on the grace of God, to be more than ever attentive to personal religion, and fervent and unceasing prayer; to consecrate themselves afresh to the service of the Great Head of the Church; to give themselves more fully to the work of love and charity, to invite and encourage the wanderers; particularly to attend all the Means of Grace, and to enjoin this important duty on the members of our Classes; to be more stirred up in the discharge of our responsibilities as officers of the Church, and thus, by a life of holiness to the Lord, secure an extension and revival of His work, and the promotion of vital godliness among the people".

Rev Dr Hugh B Sherlock, who in May 1967 at the Inauguration of the Autonomous Conference of the Methodist Church in the Caribbean and the Americas (MCCA) became its first Connexional President, knew well the thrilling story: "Methodism Sailed to the Caribbean." It was his vision and perception of the providential Hand of God carrying on the work of redemption and liberation, which constrained him – together with the faithful – to seek "by God's unerring spirit," to fashion a Church and people "to serve the present age".

Though things in general are altogether different in the third millennium than they were when Methodism Sailed to the Caribbean, the saying: "Man is free, but everywhere in chains," is certainly pregnant with meaning. Rev Dr Sherlock was not unaware of the ills which bedevil our people in the islands and continents today. Mindful of the past, the Church is challenged to seize this new day of opportunity, and proclaim by word, deeds and life, "the unsearchable riches of Christ."

"Gone the days of cruel scourging.
Gone the slaver's blood–stained chains,
Now for us the Spirit's urging,
Now the love of Christ constrains,
Shout we then in acclamation,

Gladly now our chorus raise.
Mainland join our jubilation,
Islands sing in loudest praise!
Lord Thy Church its task unfinished,
Seeks Thy wisdom, grace, and power,
Let us not with strength diminished
Fail Thee in this glorious hour.
Still obedient to the vision
Of our people saved from sin,
May Thy Church pursue its mission
Till Thy sons are gathered in."

Hugh B Sherlock

Chapter 2

The Congregations and their Outreach Ebenezer: The Valley and Beyond

The Reverend Joseph R Lloyd*

Methodism was introduced to Anguilla in 1813 by John Hodge a native of the island who it is believed came under the influence of Methodism in one of the neighbouring islands of St Eustatius or St Bartholomew (St. Barths) and underwent conversion.

On his return home he was greatly dismayed to discover that the island had been without a church, a clergyman, or any form of religious instruction since the French invasion of 1796. Without delay John Hodge petitioned the Deputy Governor seeking permission to preach to the slaves. His request was granted and Hodge began to preach the gospel of salvation and liberation to the enslaved masses. From the very outset his efforts proved to be effective. In 1815 when the Rev Calverley Riley visited Anguilla he found that John Hodge was pastoring a flock of two hundred and fifty Methodists. One of the challenges which now presented itself was a lack of adequate accommodation. To obviate this

* See biographical note, page 68.

problem, the first Methodist church was erected by John Hodge at The Valley in 1815, just to the east of where Ebenezer now stands. As creditable and commendable as this effort was, the increasing numbers of slaves who gathered weekly for worship rendered the building inadequate in a few years' time. The power of the gospel to change and transform lives was being evidenced.

In 1817, a circular written by two Methodist members of the British Parliament was addressed to prominent officials in the West Indies seeking information with regard to the social and moral conditions of the islands and the work of the missionaries. In response the Deputy Governor of Anguilla wrote: "The unexpected introduction of religion took place in 1813 in which year I received a letter from John Hodge a free coloured man and a native of this island importuning my sanction for the establishment of it. Deeming it essential to the reformation of the slaves who, before that period, were conducting themselves in habitual violation of the whole system of morality, and with a view to discipline them in their duty to God and man, I readily offered every encouragement to the petitioner to discharge his duties as a Local Preacher without the most trifling procrastination, until Class Meetings were established to investigate them which duties he still continues to discharge."

Shortly after establishing Methodism in Anguilla, Hodge made several visits to St Maarten/St Martin and preached on both the French and Dutch parts of the island. These tours were very successful. As a result, Methodism took root in St Maarten/St Martin and flourished following its inception in 1817. The Lt Governor of St Maarten wrote this letter in praise of John Hodge who established Methodism on the island.

"I beg leave to proceed to state that salutary effects of religion in the island of St Maarten were occasioned by John Hodge's unwearied attention and perseverance. It is an island, peopled with an ungodly people, who were strong and powerful enemies to the Methodist Religion, which they ever held in contempt. But divine providence seemed in a great measure to be instrumental and to make John Hodge strong and daring to establish the Gospel in St Maarten, and to add to his fervent zeal in promoting the glory of God. Thus after many Missionary attempts to settle in that island, which proved vain, God saw meet to display his wonders through John Hodge, in bringing into complete condescension the people in St Maarten to bow with submission to His will." (Biography of John Hodge by Kenn Banks – 28 April, 2002).

In a letter to the Wesleyan Mission House, UK, on 27 October 1824, Hodge reported that sixty converts were added to the church during the year, and sixteen or seventeen were whites. In a subsequent letter of 26 May 1826, Hodge alluded to the overcrowding of the church at The Valley: "The church is always crowded and is much too small, more than a few being obliged to stand without every Sabbath Day. Indeed, there is no one house in the eleven different places I preach that can hold all the people at any one time."

By now outreach work had reached as far as South Hill, four miles west of The Valley – the original point where the work was begun. Numerically the converts increased phenomenally and there was much difficulty in procuring any house large enough to meet the need. Assisted by the slaves, Hodge began to build a wooden church. When he wrote to the Mission House on 15th June 1827 he reported on the progress of the work on the church. Unfortunately, Hodge, who by this time had become an ordained minister in the Methodist Church, was transferred before its completion. Hodge's next letter was written to the Wesleyan Mission House on 29 September 1827. He rejoiced as he reported an increase of 120 members.

The work which Hodge had begun and laboured tirelessly to maintain and expand was entrusted into the hands of Henry Britten, a young English missionary who arrived in Anguilla on 20 February 1828. His letters and diaries are very enlightening in giving insights into the work of the church. In a letter to the Wesleyan Mission House on the 23 May 1828 Britten observed: "Agreeable to the Conference appointment, we have succeeded Brother Hodge in Anguilla. We find the general state of the Society as good as we expected. There is a prospect of much good, but the good work is not a little retarded by the want of room to accommodate the people whose wish it is to hear the gospel as preached by your missionaries. We have at present 300 members in the society. Our church is 36 feet by 21 feet which is not more than half large enough comfortably to seat those who are actually in connection with us. We have several hundred children committed with our schools but no accommodation for them. They never have an opportunity of being present at public worship. This I deeply regret."

Britten impressed upon the Mission House how requisite financial help would be in accelerating the building of the new church at The Valley. At that time he was faced with stiff competition from an Anglican clergyman who had been sent to the island to erect a church. Alluding to this, Britten said that he had started a Sunday School and Day School and was attracting many of our most promising students. He had already received one thousand pounds from the government to build the church and had the support of many planters. Britten expressed concern that when construction began on the Anglican Church all the best mechanics and artisans would be occupied there leaving none for the construction of the new church. Britten used this argument to instil some urgency in the Missionary Society to contribute financially toward the erection of the new church.

Early in his tenure in Anguilla, Britten focused his attention on the erection of a new church at The Valley because the existing church had become small, the completion of the church at The Road, the procuring of a second missionary and continued outreach. These projects were tackled with great zeal and determination. This extract from his letter to the Wesleyan Mission House dated 23 May 1828 speaks of Britten's firm conviction of the dire necessity for a church at The Road. "It is desirable, yea it is necessary for the prosperity and extension of the cause among us, that there should be a church and Missionary at The Road who would be able to attend to the people residing 12 or more miles distant from me and whom I can scarcely preach to once a month and never or very rarely can pay them a pastoral visit, not even in cases of affliction. There are doors of usefulness open to me which I cannot enter for want of time, having an appointment for every day in the week."

In his letter of 20 November 1828, Britten alluded to the completion and dedication of the new church at The Road: "The committee will be glad to hear that we have now completed a most substantial little church 36 feet by 21 feet and there is no debt remaining. I have secured accommodation for 190 Sunday School children. Matters are so arranged that if at any subsequent period a larger church be requisite, one may be built on the land we have – it being a quantity sufficient – and the present without any inconvenience be made a Mission House. On Wednesday the 12th November 1828 the new Wesleyan Methodist Church at The Road (Coke Church) was solemnly dedicated to the worship of Almighty God."

In his journal for 25 July 1830, Britten gives the following account of the newly constructed Ebenezer Church. "The church at The Valley is finished, at least so far as to be consecrated to divine worship. It was opened on Sunday 25th July 1830. Several weeks previous notice had been given, and great interest was excited in the minds of our dear people and in the colony generally. My most sanguine expectations were excited, but the events of the day happily more than exceeded them all. The day was delightfully cool and pleasant and at an early hour in the morning the people were seen in every direction bending their course to the sacred edifice. Long before the time appointed for the commencement of the service, the cool commodious building was crowded to excess. Such congregations were never before witnessed on any occasion in this colony, and their behaviour throughout was marked with the greatest possible decorum and seriousness."

Britten never succeeded in getting the Mission House in London to station a second minister on the island even though he was persistent with such a request. "I believe there is a loud call from Providence for the labours of a second missionary in the island. The extent of labours from east to west is nearly 20 miles. We have a society of 600 members scattered over this distance. There are 10 estates accessible by me and on 6 of which we may have schools similar to those we established in Antigua." Britten laments: "If our people were not so poor that they can contribute little to the support of the cause, how soon would even Anguilla petition for a second missionary? The harvest is truly great, but the labourers are few. O may the Lord in due time send another labourer in this part of His vineyard!" One hundred and sixty-six (166) years elapsed before Henry Britten's vision for the need of a second minister in Anguilla materialized.

History was made in the Anguilla Circuit when on 1 September 1994 the Rev Keith B Lewis took up his appointment as circuit minister. His tenure lasted merely one year as he was transferred to the British Virgin Islands circuit. His successor was the Rev Theophilus Nathaniel Rolle. Two ministers continued to be stationed in the circuit until the end of the 2001–2002 connexional year.

Presently, Rev Lindsay K Richardson, Superintendent, is the only minister officially appointed to the circuit due to the acute shortage of ministers in the connexion. It is anticipated that as soon as this temporary problem is resolved, the circuit will return to normal staffing.

In several of Britten's letters, mention is made of the conducting of services all over the island and regular prayer meetings in Stoney Ground which was 'far in the woods' and East End. Stories of the conversion of slaves and influential whites are also told.

In his letter of 20 November 1828 Britten writes: "Seven miles eastward of our residence we have a society of nearly 50 persons whom I can with difficulty meet once a quarter to give them their tickets. To the westward of us ten miles there is another society of about 40 in similar circumstances." This latter reference would be to West End.

Reference is made elsewhere of Britten preaching in a small house at East End. It would appear that the society that was formed seven miles eastward of Britten's residence was at Mt Fortune.

Britten also makes mention of preaching at Mt Pleasant Estate, somewhere in the vicinity of Rey Hill. He remarked that he did not expect to find such an estate in Anguilla. 113 slaves resided on this estate and the manager's house was the venue for the service.

On 4 March 1828 Britten preached at Blowing Point, which he estimated to be 5 miles from The Valley, and conducted evening service at the Secretaries' House. He described the congregation as being large and seriously attentive. Sometime in the following week he alluded to his visit on Col Hodges estate to visit a Catechist who had taken seriously ill.

It is interesting to discover that Britten refers to the Clergyman being present. The Clergyman was the Anglican priest who had been sent to Anguilla to establish a church. Initially, relationships between him and Britten were not very cordial. There was constant conflict between them. He did not seem to accept and recognize Britten as a fellow preacher of the gospel. This affected air seemed to have been changing for the better. This is confirmed by this remark made by Britten. "The clergyman with his lady called after me today. He was very sociable and seemed to regard me as a fellow labourer. We parted with mutual expressions of affection and hopes of being blessed to each other."

Prior to his departure from Anguilla in 1830, Britten made reference to the society eastward of The Valley and the plans which were being made to build a church. These plans never materialized. To date there is no organized Methodist work east of Ebenezer beyond The Valley area.

One of the formidable challenges that confronted Ebenezer and the antecedent congregation in an attempt at outreach was the provision of formal education for the slaves. This task was made more difficult because the owners of the plantations resisted such a move vigorously.

On 26 May 1826, John Hodge alludes to the establishment of a day school and his superintendency of it. "My work now is to preach 5 times a week, superintend the school and meet one or two classes, besides catechizing the children in different places." He further stated: "It might be needful to say with respect to a day school, there is a young white man here, a member of Society of a respectable family and much respected by all the people being known to be strictly moral from a child . . . who may be employed with great advantage. If the Committee think proper we should and can afford to give him 100 pounds sterling. He is now teaching school for the support of himself, mother and sister and is our Sunday School teacher." Hodge showed keen interest in the school and decided to send his own son.

In a letter dated 23 May 1828, Britten speaks about several hundred children committed with our schools but no accommodation for them. He also refers to the Anglican clergyman from Barbados who has established a good day school to which the catechist's whole time is devoted.

He expressed concern that a number of children had left the Methodist school to attend the Anglican school. The schools were available to adults and children, e.g., mention is made of two Adult schools containing about 70 persons and a Thursday evening school containing nearly the same number of children and adults. The prospects for the establishment of schools on the estates got better and better. Britten observes: "There are 10 estates accessible by me on 6 of which we may have schools similar to those we established in Antigua. Under existing circumstances I shall scarcely ever be able to visit an estate. I have a leaders' meeting to attend every week, two churches to preach in – a large evening school to attend – which I cannot leave to Mrs B in consequence of there being a number of wild unruly young persons of both sexes attached to it."

After the abolition of slavery in 1834, many Anguillians migrated to some of the neighbouring islands in search of a better livelihood. The educational background which they had received proved advantageous.

Long after Emancipation, Ebenezer continued to offer educational opportunities. For many years the church served a dual purpose – a place of worship on Sunday and school from Monday to Friday. In 1915, the government assumed full responsibility for education in Anguilla. By this time the school had been housed in a separate building which was owned by the church and rented by the government. At the beginning of the 1970–71 school year, the church building which housed the government school was vacated by government and the pupils entered the Valley Primary School – a government owned building. The impact exerted by Ebenezer in the educational, social and cultural spheres enhanced people's lives and equipped them for obtaining the best out of life in their immediate community and beyond.

Up to the end of the first half of the 20th century Ebenezer was in the vanguard of social organization and outreach. Few other agents or organizations were involved in such a way. The church still continues to offer programmes in social expansion and outreach.

The valiant efforts at expansion and outreach did not result in the permanent planting of congregations eastwards beyond The Valley area. However, these attempts awakened a great zeal and enthusiasm on the part of members of Ebenezer to boost and strengthen the existing work. Right down through the years there have been a noble band of stewards, local preachers, class leaders, and Sunday School teachers who, through commitment and training, have worked with groups within the church, equipping them for life and ministry. Committed lay preachers proclaimed the gospel not only from pulpits within the church but took to the community and beyond with Open Air Meetings regularly. There was neither electricity nor public address systems in those early days to facilitate seeing and hearing, but people left the confines of their homes and supported the work. Cottage meetings at the homes of the sick and shut-in helped to promote fellowship and offer spiritual care.

From the inception of Methodism in the Caribbean and the Americas in 1760, laypersons have played a crucial role in the expansion and outreach of the church. With diligence, commitment, and zeal, they laboured tirelessly to consolidate and expand the work. Local stalwarts and pioneers like Richard Hazel, Tom Markham, Obed Anthony, William Claxton and William Powell expended countless hours in propagating Methodism. Verse 2 of Charles Wesley's hymn (MHB 263) gives an apt description of John Hodge's labours in the early years of the inception of Methodism in Anguilla:

> *"When He first the work begun,*
> *Small and feeble was His day;*
> *Now the word doth swiftly run,*
> *Now it wins its widening way;*
> *More and more it spreads and grows*
> *Ever mighty to prevail;*
> *Sin's strongholds it now o'erthrows,*
> *Shakes the trembling gates of hell."*

A cursory glance at the development of Methodism in Anguilla, particularly in the latter half of the 20th century, highlights the prominence of the activity of laypersons in the expansion and outreach process. Constraints upon me particularly with regard to space will preclude me from compiling an exhaustive list. However, I will attempt to showcase the names of some persons whom I knew and who were associated with me personally, or of whom I learnt about: Dr Alfred McDonald, Richard James Lloyd, Sis Rose Rogers (Aunt Rose), Sis Octavia Richardson (Cousin Tavi), Sis Louisa Ann Richardson (Tan), Sis Rose Carter (Tr Rose), Sis Ruby Carter (Tr Ruby), Sis Inez Brooks (Iney), Sis Geraldine Gumbs, Mr & Mrs George Roberts, Bro Peter Richardson (Pete), Mr & Mrs Walter Richardson, Sis Caroline Gumbs, Mr & Mrs Charles Lloyd, Bro Kenneth Banks (Kenn), Bro Sanford Richardson.

The majority of persons whose names have been aforementioned have now joined the Church Triumphant. I join with the apocryphal writer of Ecclesiasticus 44: 7–10 (or The Wisdom of Jesus, the Son of Sirach) in declaring:

7. "All these were honoured in their generations,
   and were the glory of their times,

8. There are some of them who have left a name, so that men
   declare their praise.

9. And there are some who have no memorial,
   Who have perished as though they have not lived; they have
   become as though they had not been born, and so have their
   children after them.

10. But these were men of mercy, whose righteous deeds have not
    been forgotten."

Organizations like the Boy Scouts, Boys' Brigade, Youth Fellowship, Girls' Brigade, Men's Fellowship and Women's Groups did much to promote social and cultural outreach and spiritual formation. Outreach through the Sunday School helped to promote the sense of belonging to one another and to Christ. This resulted from the corporate activity which was effected.

Many persons who held or are presently filling key positions in public or private life, attribute their success partially to the discipline which was inculcated in them and the sound instruction which they received from the church. Ebenezer has always been in the forefront of social organization and outreach in the community.

A large number of politicians, ministers of religion, medical practitioners, public speakers look back with pride and gratitude to those early years in their lives when, affiliated with one or more organizations in the church, they were coached in public speaking, conducting of meetings etc., which inspired and motivated them in later years to pursue their vocations or careers. It must be noted that these activities were not confined to adherents and members of Ebenezer alone. The wider community was afforded the opportunity to participate

Despite the commendable and persistent efforts of John Hodge and his successors to plant new congregations in The Valley and beyond, no traces have remained of the nascent congregations that had been formed in the eastern section of the island. However, on the western part of the island where a significant impact had also been made, congregations have survived (though not housed in the original buildings) at South Hill and West End.

In St Maarten/St Martin, where from his base in The Valley, John Hodge was instrumental in planting Methodism, very strong congregations still function at Cole Bay, Philipsburg (Dutch side) and Marigot (French side).

Evangelism, Mission and Outreach remain a challenge for the

church in every age and generation. There will always be unconquered territory and open doors which we must have the conviction and the courage to enter.

Our forebears have left us a rich heritage. May we do our utmost to maintain and uphold all that is noble and good in that heritage so that in due course generations yet unborn may enter into our labours.

The prayer of George Wallace Briggs is timely and germane:

"They [our forebears] reaped not where they laboured
We reap what they have sown
Our harvest may be garnered
By ages yet unknown.
The days of old have dowered us
With gifts beyond all praise:
Our Father, make us faithful
To serve the coming days."
                    (MHB 979, verse 3)

Chapter 3

Bethel – The Road – and Due West

*The Reverend S Wilfred Hodge**

In 1963 the Methodist Church in Anguilla celebrated its one hundred and fiftieth Anniversary 1813–1963. The superintendent at that time was the Rev Desmond Mason and the Chairman of Leeward Islands District was the Rev Atherton Didier, BD, who once served in Anguilla from 1936–1940.

In his message to the Church in Anguilla, Rev Didier wrote: "I count it a great privilege to have served in Anguilla for four of the happiest years of my ministry. It was in Anguilla that Mrs Didier and I set up our first home after marriage. It was in Anguilla that our daughter Joan was born. We shall always be grateful for the love and kindness with which you surrounded us. We shall always thank God for the enrichment we received from our fellowship with you. What a joy and inspiration it was to see your faith and courage, to witness your deep love for Christ and His Church and to feel the strength of your loyalty to the cause of His kingdom. We knew then, without any doubt, that the flame kindled a hundred and fifty years ago was still burning brightly in the land, and

* See biographical note, page 67.

we knew, too, you were resolved by the grace of God that the flame would never be put out."

He goes on to say: "Everywhere we have gone we have held up Anguilla as a shining example of good home and family life, and of honest, industrious and courageous living. We have spoken with pride of your virile Church life, and the quality of your Christian discipleship."

In the same souvenir booklet there is a message from the then Warden of Anguilla, His Worship, V F Byron Esq, a dedicated Methodist, he wrote:

"The historic occasion gives us all a chance to pause, to look back over the years and contemplate on the impact that Methodism must have made on the people living in this small corner of the globe since its introduction 150 years ago. At once does it become apparent that the work of the Methodist Church in Anguilla and the witness of its members here, must have had as a fundamental aim the changing of the evil in human thought and conduct, and the encouraging of standards that are decent and good throughout the land. In so far as these aims have been realized through the teaching and practice of Methodists in this island, it is reasonable to believe that better citizens of the community have been produced as a result."

The Rev Didier spoke of the flame that was lit 150 years ago, and Mr Byron spoke of the witness of the Methodist Church in Anguilla and its fundamental aim changing of the evil in human thought and conduct.

The flame was lit by one, John Hodge, in the year 1813. There is no record as to where John Hodge came under the influence of Methodism, undoubtedly in one of the neighbouring islands, perhaps St Barths or St Eustatius. It was a time when the island had been without a Church and without a clergyman, so there was no form of religious instruction since the French invaded the island in 1796.

There seems to be no doubt that John Hodge had experienced a genuine conversion, for on his return to Anguilla, he began to bear witness to Christ. His testimony bore fruit for many were converted to the faith. It was in the providence of God that he came to the island as a converted Methodist, to plant the seeds of the Methodist faith and to see it grow and blossom.

John Hodge assumed the responsibility of local preacher. Apart from his preaching ministry, he was also administrator; he appointed class leaders to lead the classes which he established from among his converts.

What is outstanding was the impact the Methodist witness had on the social life of the people. The Deputy Governor of Anguilla, in response to a Circular written by two Methodist members of the British

Parliament seeking information as to the social and moral conditions of the islands and the work of Missionaries, wrote:

> "The unexpected introduction of religion took place in the year 1813 in which I received a letter from John Hodge, a free coloured man and a native of the island importuning my sanction for the establishment of it. Deeming it essential to the reformation of the slaves who before that period, were conducting themselves in habitual violation of the whole system of morality and with a view to discipline them in their duty to God and man, I readily offered every encouragement to the petitioner."

Rev James Whitworth visited Anguilla from St Barths and recorded the testimony of a resident proprietor who formerly was prejudiced against Methodism, "Since its coming, there has been an almost entire cessation of dancing, wakes and carousing among the slaves; they enjoy good health and have scarcely any need for doctors."

John Hodge bore his witness with confidence and conviction that in a matter of two years, in 1815, when Rev Calverley Riley visited Anguilla he found a Methodist community of two hundred and fifty.

On his recommendation, John Hodge was officially appointed a Lay Agent, and in 1818 the Anguilla Circuit appeared on the list of stations with 169 members and the promise of a minister to be sent.

The Rev Henry Britten, a young English missionary who succeeded the Rev John Hodge, was responsible for the erection of a church at The Road that measured 36feet by 21feet. The Road Church had a congregation of 200 members and a Sunday School of about 100 children. Henry Britten believed the membership would double and the School treble if there was a resident missionary. The foundation of the first church at The Road can still be seen in the old cemetery, not far from the present church.

By the time slavery was abolished in 1834, the membership of the Methodist Church in Anguilla had grown to 617 due in no small part to a most original and earnest preacher, Rev Matthew Banks whose ministry in Anguilla was eminently successful.

Shortly after the Emancipation of the slaves many Anguillians drifted to other islands in search of a better livelihood, and the shrinkage of the population affected the work of the church. The membership dwindled to the point where the Church was unable to support a minister. The Rev George Croft, the last in the succession of resident ministers, was withdrawn for this very reason. From 1837–1867, there was no resident minister in Anguilla.

The work was maintained by the faithful and dedicated service of lay people. A minister from a neighbouring island visited once per quarter to renew tickets of membership, administer the Sacraments, pay pastoral visits, hold Leaders' Meetings, exercise discipline and admit new members. But as conditions improved, the work of the Church also improved until a minister was once more appointed to the island which again became a separate circuit.

Most of what has so far been written could be applied to the entire island, but this part of the story is about Bethel Church at The Road, and Immanuel at West End. The story of Bethel begins with the illustrious name of Rev Dirk Almair Schouten who, after serving as a lay agent for several years, was accepted for the ministry in 1879 especially for work in Anguilla. Although he served the entire island as parson, schoolmaster, doctor, he is specifically associated with the building of the Methodist Church at The Road in the year 1878, an edifice that is considered one of the most beautiful buildings on the island.

Erecting this Church was a stupendous task of no mean undertaking. In the first place there was the building material to be found and conveyed to the site. Mr Schouten went himself with his helpers to the little island called Scrub off the east end of Anguilla, and hewed the stones he needed out of the quarry. Lime was used, as cement was not easily procured and probably was not heard of. Mr Schouten himself helped with the cutting of the wood for the burning of the lime in the kiln, and no doubt helped in the procuring of the coral. Skilled workmen were not available in Anguilla in those days, so he had to use men who had never handled or used carpenters' and masons' tools before. Today as we look at his portrait we read on his face 'his holy zeal, his unremitting toil – the genius who had the infinite capacity for taking pains.'

Rev Dirk Almair Schouten laboured for forty-two years proclaiming the Gospel in Anguilla. He has been described as "one of the saintliest men Methodism ever possessed." As someone described him: "Look at his photo; notice the lines of labour, care and sorrow. How humble, patient and determined he seems". He built a magnificent edifice with his own hands, yet at the same time built a community of believers whose witness has spanned the years."

The people of Anguilla must never be allowed to forget the unselfish devotion, the heroic labours and the blameless ministry of the Rev Dirk Almair Schouten who, after the fire which destroyed the Manse, lived next to Bethel Church before transferring to Tortola where he died in 1909. He has left behind us a great legacy. A plaque erected to his honour stands at the Bethel Church. Three of his children who survived him lived in the house next to the Bethel Church which once served as a manse: Sarah Schouten was organist at Bethel for over forty years and was renowned for her delicious baking; Miss Lil, as she was affectionately known, became head-teacher at West End – one could see her travelling each morning in her buggy, drawn by a horse; and Miss Babe was the keen gardener. They like many others of their generation were the bulwarks of the Methodist witness at The Road.

Among the ministers who served the Methodist Church in the following years, special mention, however, must be made of the work of the Rev A B B Baker. It was during his ministry, 1924–34, that The Road Church was enlarged. Just as the congregation had grown too large for the first church built by Rev Britten in 1828, so, with the passing of the years, the second Church proved inadequate for the congregation. In 1927, Mr Baker formed at The Road, the Ladies Aid Society, which under his courageous leadership succeeded in raising the funds for the greatly needed work of enlargement. The actual work was successfully carried through in 1934 by the Rev George E Lawrence. The Chairman of the District at that time was the Rev William Sunter, and it was through his building experience and expertise that the intricate expansion took place. Bethel congregation is greatly indebted to these gentlemen

Outstanding persons who served the Bethel Congregation during the twentieth century were Karen Richardson, better known as Teacher K., who served as Local Preacher, Class Leader, Superintendent of the Sunday School; Muriel Richardson who took over as organist after the death of Sarah Schouten, and served in that post for many years; her mother, Louisa Richardson; J B Owen, Anguilla's philanthropist, serving the Church as Local Preacher and Circuit Steward for many years; Octavia Daniel, Francis and Lillian Hodge, Sarah Carty of Blowing Point, Jefferson Gumbs, Glossandra Dollison, and many others who were bulwarks in their day and held the Church together during difficult times.

Ministers who served after the departure of Rev Schouten served the entire island, but lived in the Manse which was now situated at the entrance to Sandy Ground. When that Manse was damaged in a hurricane and was no longer serviceable, a new manse was erected at South Hill adjacent to Bethel Church.

Bethel congregation served five immediate communities, Upper and Lower South Hill, Blowing Point, Sandy Ground and North Hill, but many persons travelled from West End and Long Bay to attend worship at The Road. These were days when there were no vehicles, and persons walked every Sunday these long distances to attend worship in the morning, and the children would return for Sunday School, and some would even return for the evening service. They also walked these long distances for weddings and for funerals, at times in the heat of the midday sun. The Methodist Church was the only religious body serving this entire section of the island in the early part of the twentieth century.

It would only be a matter of time before there sprung up in each of these communities, Sunday Schools, to meet the needs of the growing number of children who refused to take the long trek to Bethel. Sunday Schools were started in Blowing Point, North Hill, Sandy Ground and Lower South Hill. These Sunday Schools originally met in homes.

Older persons began to find the long journey to Bethel beyond their physical capabilities, and there was a crying need to provide opportunities for worship and service in these communities.

Blowing Point

The first of these was Blowing Point. Blowing Point Village is situated some three to four miles from Bethel. Sunday School was started at Blowing Point by Eliza Romney and was held under a mahogany tree. Allan and Ilva Romney who ran a rum shop in the community gave a portion of the rum shop to house the Sunday School! Urban Hazel was the Superintendent, ably assisted by Eliza Romney and Camelia Hodge.

The Hall was also used for evening worship and for confirmation classes. There was need for a permanent presence of the Methodist Church in the community, so the search began for a piece of land to erect a building. This land was obtained from Louisa Hughes, and the members began to gather stones and other material for the erection of a building. The design for the building was done by the resident Roman Catholic priest. Work began on the building in 1965 during the ministry of Rev Martin Roberts. Johnson Hodge of The Valley Church laid the foundation and the building was completed by Frederick Richardson of Long Bay. Joseph Romney and his wife were able to mobilize the community, and they both worked relentlessly to see the building completed.

On 3 February 1967, during the year of the Anguilla revolution, the Blowing Point Methodist Church was completed and dedicated to the glory of God. At this time the annual District Synod was meeting in St Maarten/St Martin, and the entire Synod ferried to Anguilla for the occasion, and marched joyfully from the pier to the Church with singing for the dedication of the new structure.

John Mac Connor and Eliza Romney were the first two stewards, the latter being replaced by Viola Connor who was also the Sunday

School Superintendent and a Class Leader. Other leaders included Camelia Hodge, Sylvanus Davis, Cordelia Connor, John MacConnor, Magdalyn Gumbs, and Viola Smith.

The first preachers of Blowing Point were Janet Davis, Maycille Romney Roberts, followed by Carmen Romney and Norma Bennett Maccow. More recent is Wendell Samuel Connor.

For some time the Society was without a name and in 1978 it was given the name "Maranatha". The congregation has served the community well and the membership has grown over the years. There are several groups serving the Church: Women's League, Youth Fellowship, Senior and Youth Choir and a Sunday School.

North Hill

Blowing Point was followed by North Hill. The Sunday School at North Hill was started by Colin Bynoe in the seventies and it met for many years under his leadership in a home. Shortly after the start of the Sunday School worship began in the building known as the Big House, which was later demolished by hurricane, but the congregation met there until a sanctuary was erected in 1982 during the ministry of the Revs Peterson Joseph and J Evans Dodds on land donated by the family of the Rev C L Carty. Four work teams from the United States assisted in the erection of the building and the local folk assisted in "picking rocks" and cooking and housing the members of the teams.

One of the foundation members at North Hill was Connie Gumbs, who was choir director and organist as well as Class Leader. Yolande McDonald started the annual Bazaar, Codvis Connor started the Women's League and was the first President. Her post was taken over by Marjorie Gumbs. Mention needs to be made of Olympia Gumbs who served as Class leader, member of the Women's League and Church Caretaker. Presently there is a Girls' Brigade Company, a Youth Group, a Young Adult Group called Zion Adventurers, a Senior Choir and a Women's League.

Sandy Ground

One can stand at Bethel Church, The Road, look over the hill and see the small village of Sandy Ground, nestled between the salt pond and The Road harbour. The salt pond was the mainstay of Anguilla's economy for many years, but the business has since declined.

Sandy Ground has always been a Methodist community, and the folk travelled up the hill to School, Church and Sunday School.

Sometimes twice on Sunday they would tread up the hill. Many devoted members of Bethel hailed from Sandy Ground: Glossandra Dollison (Teacher Glossy), Octavia Daniel who ran a small library in her little cottage, Averil Carty, the mother of one of our Methodist Ministers, Rev Hugo Rey, Meredith Carty and Ursula Hughes.

It was in 1983, that Daisy Carty, mother of another Methodist Minister, Rev Erica Carty, started a Sunday School which met at the back porch of her home. About twenty children attended, including one adult.

On 11 June 1986, Rev Richard Brownwhale began holding evening service in a hall owned by Edwin and Daisy Carty and loaned to the Church for that purpose. Morning worship began 6.30 am on 2 June 1991 during the ministry of the Rev John A Gumbs, a son of the soil. There were about forty persons in attendance. The members maintained their membership at Bethel. At the same time, the Sunday School began meeting in the Hall under the leadership of Daisy Carty.

Sandy Ground officially became a Society in 1994. The following were appointed leaders of Classes: Meredith Carty, Leonie Richardson, Signa Richardson, Pearl Connor, Daisy Carty, Elvarie Carty and Edwin Carty, whose class was later taken over by Lindsay Richardson, father of Rev Keithley Richardson. Leonie Richardson, Daisy Carty, Irenee Richardson and Louise Hazel were stewards. Daisy Carty and Lindsay Richardson became fully accredited preachers.

In 2000, the Hall was rebuilt and redesigned; the members, led by Edwin Carty, with the help of the circuit provided the material and labour and the present lovely edifice was dedicated on February 25, 2001 during the ministry of Rev Joseph Lloyd. At the dedication ceremony, the title to the land was handed over to the Church, a gift from Edwin Carty and family.

This small congregation of about eighty members now have an active choir, started by Veronica Gumbs, wife of Rev John A Gumbs, now under the directorship of Jean Hodge, wife of Rev Dr S Wilfred Hodge, a Women's League and a Youth Fellowship.

West End and Long Bay

There are no specific dates available as to when the Methodist witness came to the western end of the island to the communities of Long Bay and West End. The fact that those two communities were for many years served solely by the Methodist Church is indicative of the fact that Methodism was planted there during the time of slavery. The Rev Britten in 1828 makes reference to a society of about forty members.

But there is no reference as to the erection of a building.

While there may have been a meeting of members in homes or in the open, there is reliable information that weddings and funerals of persons from that end of the island took place at Bethel, The Road, and people walked the distance to these events. Many members from Long Bay and West End attended worship at The Road and had their membership at The Road, even after a building was erected at West End.

In the mid-nineteenth century a school was started by a Mr Dickenson who was also the headteacher of the school for many years. A cistern marking the site of that first school now serves as a look-out for boat enthusiasts. When the Methodist Church was built the school was transferred to the Methodist Church.

One of the outstanding names that has survived is Tom Hodge, great grand-father of two of the oldest members of the West End congregation living in Long Bay, Evelyn Hodge and Austin Hodge, both in their nineties. John "Waddy" Hodge's mother, Jemima Hodge, was one of the outstanding leaders of that society, she was also a local preacher, along with Julia Richardson, a class leader and Adelaide who served as Sunday School superintendent for many years.

John "Waddy" Hodge, one of Anguilla's leading personalities, not only represented his district in government but was an outstanding layperson at the West End Church, following in the footsteps of his mother. He was Local Preacher, Class Leader, Society Steward and choir director who served the Church with distinction. Another outstanding layperson was Alma Hodge Richardson who served the Church as Class Leader, Local Preacher, Women's League President, Island President, and Circuit Steward. She has also left behind a very dedicated and committed family whose members now hold many positions of leadership in the Church and one son is a cirucit steward. Jane Hodge Richardson was organist for many years as well as a teacher in the day school.

The older members recall the two great annual events of their Church, the annual harvest thanksgiving service when members of the other two congregations would walk the distance and spend the entire day sharing in this annual event. The other event was the annual Wesley Guild Rally when members from the West End congregation would walk the distance to The Road Church for the occasion.

The old Church/School building, the foundations of which still stand, was destroyed by a hurricane in 1950. Plans had already been made to replace this building which had served its purpose as school and place of worship. Its destruction was greeted with rejoicing, as though the hand of God was in it. The insurance money was surely welcomed for the construction of the new Church. Government also built a new school for the community. A long-standing and outstanding member of the Church, Ezra Richardson, along with Iman Richardson, Walter Richardson and Thomas Hodge, was responsible for the erection of the new structure during the ministry of the Rev Donald Henry, and the building was dedicated on 5 May 1953. This year, 2003, marks the fiftieth anniversary of the building with plans to replace the present structure which is now too small for the growing congregation.

The Methodists of West End and Long Bay have remained loyal to their church over the years and continue to make an invaluable contribution to the Methodist witness. There is an active Sunday School, a Youth Fellowship, a Women's League and a Senior Choir.

Chapter 4

The Impact of Anguilla's Methodism on the Caribbean

The Reverend John A Gumbs*

On Sunday, 28 April 2002, a memorial plaque was unveiled in honour of the Anguillian born Rev John Hodge on the site where he had built the first Methodist Church (Ebenezer) in Anguilla in 1815. At the same time, the donors, the Anguilla Archaeological and Historical Society, had a similar plaque nailed on the present Ebenezer church, which was built by the slaves and dedicated in 1830. The membership had outgrown the walls of the first Church, which was now converted to serve as the Manse.

The event memorializing the birth of the two Churches is of two-fold significance. On the one hand, the first Ebenezer reminds us that John Hodge, the founder of Methodism in Anguilla, was at that time a layman, and laymen in Anguilla have ever since taken an active role in the upkeep of the Church and the propagation of the Gospel. On the other hand, the second Ebenezer is the cradle, which in more recent

* See biographical note, page 65.

years has nurtured five ministers, four of whom are now supernumerary ministers viz Rev John A Gumbs, Rev Franklin A Roberts, Rev Cecil O A Weekes and the Rev Joseph R Lloyd. The Rev E Dunstan Richardson, Superintendent Minister in the St Croix Circuit, is also from the Ebenezer Church.

The impact of Anguilla's Methodism on the Caribbean, has to be viewed from these two perspectives vis-à-vis that of the layman and that of the ordained ministry.

The Layman

The Methodist Church in the West Indies started with a layman and came to be known as the friend of the slaves and the poor. Nathaniel Gilbert, wealthy landowner, was converted by the preaching of John Wesley while on a visit to England. On his return to Antigua he started preaching to the slaves on his plantation.

How Methodism spread to the other islands has not been documented, but there is no doubt that the movement of converted slaves played an important part.

Donald Ching in his book "For Ever Beginning" wrote:

"There is a recognizable pattern in the development of the Methodist Church in the West Indies during the past two (2) centuries: The spear-head is nearly always a layman (the Gilberts and Baxters): then comes the Minister to organize, establish and extend the work (the Cokes, Warreners, Clarkes, Hammetts), then again the work, thus established and extended is maintained and perfected in the witness and pastoral exercise of laymen (the Alleys and Campbells).

In Anguilla, we know that the Methodist Church was started by John Hodge in 1813. How John Hodge became a Methodist we do not know. We do know however, that among other things he used to fight cocks. Cock-fighting has always been a hobby of the French in these islands and it is just possible that on a cock-fighting excursion to St Barths he came under the influence of the Methodist witness there, and was converted. We also know that after his conversion he stopped cock-fighting.

There are others, however, who think that his conversion was the result of the strong witness of Methodism in St Eustatius. The old dictum "The blood of the martyr is seed of the church", seems to have been operative in St Eustatius. Governor Rennels, the Governor of St

Eustatius, in an attempt to stamp out the budding Methodist witness started by a slave, Harry – affectionately known as Black Harry – issued an edict in 1788, which as Dr Coke mentioned "is the first instance known among mankind of a persecution openly avowed against religion itself. The persecution among the heathen was supported under the pretence that the Christians brought in strange gods; those among the Roman Catholics were under the pretext of the Protestants introducing heresies into the church. But this edict is openly and avowedly against Prayer the great key to every blessing".

In defiance of this unreasonable edict, Black Harry was mercilessly flogged by Isaac de Lion in a park that until this day is beautifully kept in his memory, then dragged to the jail and soon afterwards banished from the island. But! The blood of the martyr is seed of the church. Govenor Rennels died in 1811, and in that same year the membership jumped from 40 to 246. His daughter later became a Leader and was as zealous in promoting Methodism as her father had been in destroying it. It is around this time, it is believed, that John Hodge's conversion took place and he immediately returned home to propagate the Gospel. Being himself a black man and a layman, black slaves would easily identify themselves with him. He had no difficulty for example in building Ebenezer Church in 1815. Even after his ordination to the itinerant ministry in 1822, the process of identification would still be a strong contributing factor in lay participation.

It is worthy of note, that wherever John Hodge laboured, the Methodist Church is very strong, and laymen have been prominent not only in the exercise of their Pastoral duties but their civic responsibilities as well. Ministerial manpower would never be able to meet the need of all the churches in Circuits, such as British Virgin Islands, St Maarten/St Martin, St Kitts, were it not for the loyal band of local preachers and class leaders. From a civic point of view it is heartening to recognize that Methodists have been in the forefront piloting their people from universal suffrage to independence, or some other form of self-government.

In St Kitts at the time of independence the Prime Minister, Dr Kennedy Simmonds, now Dr The Right Honourable Kennedy Simmonds was Methodist. So also was the first Governor, Sir Milton Allen, followed by Sir Probyn Inniss who was followed by Sir Clement Arrindell, all Methodists. Today, the Chief Justice of the Eastern Caribbean, Sir Dennis Byron is a practicing Methodist, so also is the Governor of St Maarten, Mr Franklin Richards. Methodists have all been leaders of Government business, and in Tortola, at one time, all Ministers of Government were Methodist.

The surge in civic responsibility stems from the fact that from its infancy the Methodist Church took a keen interest in education. Church buildings were also schools and with limited financial support the church sought to educate the slaves. In addition to formal education – reading, writing and arithmetic – the church by its very structure, tended to the intellectual development of its members. The Sunday school not only taught its children through its catechism the basic teaching of the church, but also by its programmes taught children to be unafraid by reciting before congregations. Local preaching further developed young men and women in public speaking. No wonder then, that the men who ascended the political podiums were offsprings of the Methodist Church, many of whom remain eternally grateful for the church's contribution to their lives.

In St Kitts one cannot but think of Robert Bradshaw, the liberator of his people, breaking the yoke of English Colonialism and laying the foundation for independence – Vincent Byron, the father of Chief Justice Dennis Byron, a local preacher for over forty years not only served as Warden of Anguilla, but on several occasions acted as Governor of the independent state of St Kitts/Nevis – Sir Cecil Jacobs who served as Governor of the Eastern Caribbean Central Bank and is still a member of the Methodist Church in the Caribbean and the Americas (MCCA) Trust Corporation – Mr C F Henville, a solicitor who served as Vice President of the MCCA or Sir Probyn Inniss (a lawyer) former Governor of St Kitts/Nevis and a former Vice President of the MCCA.

On and on we can go enumerating a host of witnesses in St Kitts who look back in gratitude to the witness and labours of the Methodist Church to the slaves, their forbears. The Jacobs' family for example who apart from Sir Cecil (previously mentioned) also gave to our church the second Deaconess in our District, the Rev Sister Althea, now deceased, as well as her deceased brother Dr Ersdale Jacobs. Or we can think of Joe Hughes, former Warden of Anguilla, and still attends our Leeward Islands District Conference, or the Ottley family, with Dr Clive serving the community as obstetrician, and a host of others all giving dedicated service to both church and community.

What we see emerging in St Kitts is symptomatic for all the other places where John Hodge worked. In Tortola for example, one is constrained to think of Lavity Stoutt, now deceased, who for years was Chief Minister and at the same time Methodist local preacher and a representative on several occasions to the District Synod – or think of Joseph Archibald, QC, a lawyer of no mean order, and who gives freely of his expertise as Legal Counsel to the Trust Corporation and to the

Connexional Conference of the MCCA, or Charles Wesley Turnbull, a Tortolan now Governor of the American Virgin Islands, and other members of the Turnbull family all proud of their slave heritage. Or think of the Wheatleys, the O'Neals, Vanterpools, Laymen, were all devoted to their church.

In St Maarten, Claude Wathey, though not a regular worshipper, never hesitated to let you know he was a Methodist. He was responsible for Government business and was the father of the economic growth and prosperity of St Maarten. St Maarten also owes him a debt of gratitude for giving unqualified support to the Church's experimental educational project, the Methodist Agogic Centre, which used the mother tongue as the vehicle of education.

Vance James, who apart from being a local preacher, class leader, society steward, political leader has also maintained and still maintains an unusually high-performance educational/devotional programme on the radio. All these can be seen as modern day followers of John Hodge who started Methodism in St Maarten/St Martin. Nor can we forget the Labours of Sister Browlia Maillard, local preacher, class leader, educator, or that of Sister Glorine Richardson and Mammie, who for years religiously kept a Sunday School under the tamarind tree, which later mushroomed and developed into the present St Peter's church. While that was happening to the west of Philipsburg. on the east, the Meyers and the Rombleys were doing a similar thing, which has given rise to the Sucker Garden Church. Dutch St Maarten has had a cadre of devoted Methodists – the Illidges, the Hazels, the James', both in Philipsburg and Cole Bay, the Vlauns and the Bells. From the time John Hodge planted a seed of Methodism in Cole Bay under the tamarind tree, these devoted families have nurtured and watered the seed, until today it flourishes as a meaningful entity in society.

Nor is Methodism on the French side of St Martin less vibrant. Indeed, the person who approximates most closely to John Hodge was none other than Ernest Gibbs, affectionately known as Nessy or Parin. Here was a devoted Christian, who gave himself relentlessly for the propagation of the Gospel and often in a hostile climate. For over forty years, he was a most acceptable local preacher. He clothed every office in the Church (including that of Sexton) with dignity and devotion. Zealous for the spread of the Gospel, he started a church in Grand Case, and later another in Cul-de-Sac. His son, Victor, a practicing Methodist was the Chief Medical Officer for over twenty years.

The Methodist layman's socio-civic involvement in the life of our people in Anguilla is no less than it has been in the other islands where John Hodge laboured. Kenneth Hazell and David Lloyd were the

Methodist pioneers in the political arena. The baton was later taken up by Sir Emile Gumbs, Hubert Hughes, Albert Hughes, Victor Banks, Edison Baird.

When we turn to the field of education, a new era in the life of the Methodist Church began. In the year 1867, a thirty year old Methodist Minister, Rev Dirk Almair Schouten was stationed in Anguilla. He served for forty-two years and he and his family gave to the Methodist Church a head start in education and music.

In 1953, Anguilla embarked in Secondary Education – The Valley Secondary School, later to become the Albena Lake Hodge Comprehensive School. The first two Head Masters were non-Anguillians, the rest, apart from one, were not only Anguillians, but Methodists. Edison Hughes, after whom the Library at Teachers' Resource Centre is named, was the first. He was followed by St Clair Buchanan – a class leader and society steward, then by Yolande Richardson – society steward, class leader, captain of the Girls' Brigade; Rodney Rey – Circuit Steward, Society Steward and Sunday School Superintendent; Quincy Harrigan, and now Darwin Hazell. While this was going on in the school, the rest of the Education Department saw Methodists playing an active role. Elvet Hughes and Yolande Richardson as Chief Education Officers; Irma Richardson and Verna Fahie – Examination Officers; Winifred Carty and Hyacinth Hughes, Education Officers for the Primary Schools; and Adrian Hazell – Coordinator for the Primary Schools. This of course has nothing to do with the host of Methodist teachers in both our secondary and our elementary schools. When the history of education in Anguilla is written and its impact on society evaluated, the Methodist Church will have to give an account of its stewardship.

It is interesting to note that Anguilla has recently started in conjunction with the University of the West Indies, a School for Continuing Studies, and this is headed by a Methodist, Julian Harrigan. Our own local preacher, Constantine Richardson (deceased), gave invaluable service to St Kitts as Resident Tutor of the extra-mural department of The University of the West Indies, while his Anguillian wife, Dulcie Connor, OBE, headed the Teachers' Training College.

It would be remiss to overlook the contribution of Lt Col Claudius Roberts, brother of Franklin Roberts, who was responsible for setting up the Royal Anguilla Police Force. His father, Sgt George Roberts, together with a corporal and a private, maintained law and order in Anguilla for several years. Elliott Richardson, local preacher and captain of the Boys' Brigade under the watchful eye of Col Roberts, also scaled the ranks of the Royal Anguilla Police Force to become Commissioner.

In medicine, Anguilla is grateful for the invaluable contribution of Drs Lowell and Franklin Hughes – the former, a general as well as a plastic surgeon with his own medical centre, while the latter, a general physician; Dr Brett Hodge, Ob-Gyn, also with his own clinic; Dr Trevor Connor, orthodontist, also with his own clinic; Dr John Franklin, Urologist, though living in St Thomas makes himself available to Anguilla; Dr Franklin Lloyd is presently the Chief Medical Officer, while his brother, Clarence Lloyd, was the first Optometrist for St Kitts/Nevis, Anguilla.

The great-grandparents of all these devoted Methodists were either slaves or slaves who had bought their freedom. If, in all this evolution, John Hodge played a role, then Anguilla's influence cannot be underestimated. If the subject of this article were broadened to the influence of Anguilla on the Caribbean, then it is true to say that in every field of advancement, the Anglicans were as prominent as the Methodists.

In the past, Anguillians have been a migratory people. The 35 square mile low-lying island, is the most northerly of the islands in the Lesser Antilles chain. It lies about 7 miles north of St Martin and about 90 miles east of Puerto Rico. Its limestone formation means that there is very little arable land and being low lying, the rainfall is sparse – about 100 cm per year. This land offered little or no opportunity for creating a sustainable livelihood for young people. Consequently, by dint of circumstance, young people were forced to seek their fortunes abroad. Wherever they went, two things characterized the Anguillian migrant – (a) they invariably formed an Anguillian Association and (b) they became actively engaged in the life of the local Church.

Active engagement in the life of the Church meant more than being a worshipper. If, for example, no Methodist Church existed where they were, then they would try to gather the Methodists together in a house or hall to meet for worship. That is how for example the Methodist Church in Aruba began. Emile Connor, a Methodist local preacher from Anguilla, in going to Aruba to seek employment and finding no Methodist Church there, was pivotal in bringing together two other local preachers – Tom Markham from Montserrat and Richard Hazell from St Maarten, and so started the Methodist Church there. Today, the Methodist Church in Aruba is a vibrant society and has pioneered the starting of the Methodist Church in Holland. Beulah in New York, still using our Methodist hymn book, can be regarded as an Anguillian church, so strong is the Anguillian element in Beulah. The Rev A B B Baker who started the work there, when he left Beulah became the superintendent minister in Anguilla and baptized our now supernumerary minister Rev John A Gumbs. The Anguilla Society in the United

States is still active, and annually has an 'awards programme' honouring Anguillians.

In Slough, England, such is the involvement of Anguillians that for all practical purposes one can regard the churches there as Anguillian churches; Anguilla local preachers continue to preach the word. Charles Wesley would say:

> *"See how great a flame aspires*
> *Kindled by a spark of grace . . .*
>
> *When He first the work begun*
> *Small and feeble was His day*
> *Now the word doth swiftly run*
> *Now it wins its widening way*
> *More and more its spreads and grows*
> *Ever mighty to prevail*
> *Sin's strongholds it now o'erthrows*
> *Shakes the trembling gates of hell"*
> [MHB 263]

The impact of Anguilla's Methodism on the Caribbean was most decisively influenced by our laymen. They were not only local preachers but also Sunday school teachers, Women's League Presidents as well as members of the Boys' & Girls' Brigades, leaders, choristers, stewards, worshippers. They took an active interest in the life of the Church wherever they found themselves.

The Ordained Ministry

In the early days of the witness of the Methodist Church in Anguilla, the island was neatly divided into three sections – an eastern, a central and a western section. The island was further subdivided between the Anglicans and the Methodists, the two dominant denominations. The Anglicans had the eastern section, the Methodist the western section and the central section was shared by both. Tradition has it that our forefathers entered into such an agreement. We have never been able to substantiate the claim, but until this day there are no Methodist Churches in the eastern section of the island (above the Mahogany tree) and no Anglican Churches in the Western section of the island below (George Hill) although members live in each other's territory and are visited by their respective ministers and given sacrament when necessary.

When therefore we are considering the impact of the ordained ministry on the Caribbean, the Anguilla that we have to refer to is not the 35 square mile island, but only half of it. Further, when we think of population, up to about twenty years ago, we had a steady population of around 6,000. Today with the growth experienced by tourism, the population fluctuates around 11,000. Seen within the context of these two parameters – square mileage and population – Anguilla has perhaps offered more ministers to the ordained ministry of the Methodist Church than anywhere else in the Caribbean, if not in the world. The same accolade can also be given the Anglicans for their sterling contribution of thirteen sons to the priesthood of the Anglican Church in the province of the West Indies. Errol Brooks, an Anguillian, is now Bishop of the Diocese of the North Eastern Caribbean and Aruba.

Of the sixteen Methodists, two have joined the Church Triumphant – the Rev John Hodge and the Rev C Leonard Carty. The Rev John Hodge was ordained into the itinerant ministry in 1822. He was stationed in St Maarten, Tortola, St Kitts and Anguilla, and it is interesting to note that in all these islands Methodism is very strong.

The itinerant ministry of the Rev C Leonard Carty, like the rest of us, was predominantly centred in the Leeward Islands District. Anguillian ministers have served in all the Circuits. This, I would suggest, has had a homogeneous effect in the District, and perhaps might very well be the reason why the Leeward Islands District is numerically the strongest in the Connexion and financially the best structured and the most viable.

But the ordained itinerant ministry was not confined to the Leeward Islands District. Some of the brethren worked in Jamaica, Belize/Honduras, Guyana and Holland, taking with them Anguilla's flavour and fervour of Methodism. This impact is all the stronger and becomes inescapable when Brethren served as Chairmen of the following districts: Rev C Leonard Carty in the Belize/Honduras District, the Rev Franklin A Roberts and the Rev Cecil O A Weekes in the Guyana District and the Rev John A Gumbs, Rev Dr Wycherly Gumbs, Rev Joseph R Lloyd and the Rev Dr H Clifton Niles in the Leeward Islands District.

The impact of Anguilla's Methodism on Belize/Honduras and Guyana, was on one land mass; in the Leeward Islands District it touches fourteen circuits and affects the cultures of the English, Dutch, Papiemento and French speaking peoples.

The Rev Sister Vera Richardson, with fifty seven years service to her Church, was the first Deaconess in the Leeward Islands District, and her able, quiet and dignified service to her Church has had a profound influence on all those with whom she came into contact.

Our impact should also be viewed from a completely different dimension. The Rev Franklin A Roberts and Rev John A Gumbs were two in the largest batch of seven students that entered Caenwood College. The batch came to be known as "The Holy Seven".

Choosing Joshua 1: 9 in Hebrew as Caenwood's cry, The Holy Seven continued their proactive zeal in creating a crest for their blazer. The crest has now been taken over as the badge of the Methodist Church in the Caribbean and the Americas with one slight emendation, using the English text "The love of Christ constraineth us" rather than the Latin "caritas Christi urget nos". It is also noteworthy that of the seven, Evans Bailey became Chairman of the Jamaica District; Eric Clarke, Chairman of the Gambia District and later President of the Methodist Church in the Caribbean and the Americas; Franklin Roberts, Chairman of the Guyana District; and John A Gumbs, prior to becoming Chairman of the Leeward Islands District, served the Dutch church in Curacao, the Verenigde Protestantse Gemeente, where he succeeded in uniting all the Dutch reformed churches in the Netherlands Antilles and the English speaking Ebenezer church into a United Protestant Church – Unie van de Potestantse Kerken, of which he became its first President.

The Holy Seven were committed to the idea of an indigenous West Indian Church and worked towards its realization. They were also committed to the establishment of a pension fund in order to give some financial assistance to West Indian Brethren when they retired. The fund started in September 1950 when the holy seven graduated from college. Many of the older Brethren who never contributed to the fund benefited from it, and today supernumeraries receive a deeply appreciated pension.

Perhaps the greatest impact that Anguilla has made on the Caribbean is reflected in ministerial training. It is almost unthinkable that this little island would be given the responsibility for the training of our men and women within our Connexion. For about 18 years, two of our Brethren, the Rev Dr H Clifton Niles and the Rev Dr S Wilfred Hodge, have been entrusted with the responsibility of being the Methodist Ministerial Tutor/Warden at the United Theological College of the West Indies. This could not but have a positive impact on the whole of the Caribbean with the fervour of Anguilla's Methodism. This is further buttressed by the service rendered by Rev Dr Clifton Niles as Secretary for six years of the Methodist Church in the Caribbean and the Americas, a crucial period when the constitution of our church was being changed.

As you read this chapter you may be prone to ask, where on earth is Anguilla? Or, is it possible for such a tiny island to have made such a contribution to the Methodist Church? Our response is: "Come and See".

Chapter 5

Black Harry

*The Reverend Franklin A Roberts**

In telling and documenting the thrilling story of what God did in raising up the Methodist Family of Churches in England, Africa, America, the Caribbean and elsewhere, the outstanding contribution of laypersons at the very centre of operation, has often received scant recognition. We have been disinclined to sing the praises of the poor indigenous labourer in fields "white unto harvest"; of those held in bondage by the rich and powerful in society; of those whose pigment is black.

In our world come of age, revolutionary changes in social structure, and the ordering of political life have brought concepts that have impacted the Church and its mission. We have been forced to take more seriously the scriptural doctrines which we have mouthed for many a year.

In the administration and fellowship of the church, we have not always acted as though all persons are equal in the sight of the God whom we proclaim. For a long time our Methodist emphases in regard to the priesthood of all believers, and the role of laypersons in the life

* See biographical note, page 66.

of the Church have been enunciated; but our practice has seldom matched our profession.

We hail and applaud such pioneers as William Claxton and William Powell who went from Nevis – my wife's homeland – to Guyana in 1801, where they found virgin soil for the propagation of the Word; "for at that time there was no minister of Christ in the Colony." More will be said of dedicated men of vision such as Richard Hazel, who went from St Maarten and pioneered Methodist work in Aruba. The planting of our Church in Curacao centres on Obed Anthony, a Local Preacher from Dominica, who about 1930 joined the many who sought work at oil refineries in those Antillean Territories.

America and the Caribbean share a historic bond as far as Methodism is concerned. Having put the spotlight on a few black men of African stock, who in early years spent themselves in sowing the seed of the Gospel in some of our Circuits, I am moved to tell of Barbara, the cousin of Philip Embury, an Irish immigrant to America in the 1760's. I do not think that Black Harry of whom we shall take a closer look ever met this white woman face to face. He undoubtedly shared her concern for personal salvation, and getting others to know the saving grace and power of Christ and the Gospel.

Like us here in the Caribbean, Methodist immigrants, and others to America, were for a time "like sheep without a shepherd". This was primarily due to action of a Congress of American States "Declaration of Independence" on 4 July 1776. This political action not only dried up the flow of spiritual leaders from England, but also made those who remained to feel unwelcome.

It was in this kind of situation in New York, that the Irish immigrant – Philip Embury – was challenged by his cousin Barbara with the words: "If you do not preach to us, cousin, we shall all go to hell!" Embury did as she urged, and within a year a church was opened in John Street, New York, into which a thankful people moved.

I am not sure why the co-authors of this book pounced on me to write about Black Harry. Perhaps I resemble him most: "ebony in colour and tall in stature". I could not, however, say "No", to telling the story of this valiant man whose life was transformed and, thereby, enabled to stand up for his Lord through thick and thin.

It is no surprise to me that those who are caught up with the adventurous and fascinating story of Methodist beginnings – those who are arrested as they perceive the providential hand of God working for the salvation and liberation of a people enchained physically and spiritually – all find it compelling to present Black Harry as a champion for Christ who gave him the joy of present and future salvation.

In my early ministerial travel, I welcomed the opportunity to meet weekly with Methodist students in Government Schools. The period set apart was well worthwhile, and our boys found the early history and expansion of Methodism most inspiring.

I must have done a good job with the students; for on one occasion, at the beginning of the session, I was greeted "Black Harry!" Those were the days in the Caribbean when, in church and society, black was not considered "beautiful"; thus one of our brilliant ministers (not the writer) was able to say openly to the "olive skinned" District Chairman – whom he later succeeded – "you do not know what it is to be black".

Black Harry not only knew what it was to be black. He knew also what it was to be a black slave in the plantation system of his day. He knew how the black man had been uprooted from his ancestral home in Africa. He knew of the great suffering of wretched captives cooped up below deck as the "slaver" made its way through the "Middle Passage". This part of our Black History evoked anger.

Anger, however, is by no means the principal characteristic of Black Harry, whose name will forever resound with thankfulness and honour whenever the history of Methodism – particularly in St Eustatius – is considered.

In a public lecture delivered by Rev William Watty in Kingstown, St Vincent in 1991, he rightly lists Black Harry among Methodist pioneers in the Caribbean Area. He goes further to list him as one among Methodist martyrs. There has never been any doubt of Black Harry's unswerving loyalty and faithfulness to Christ, and his willingness to pay the price of Christian discipleship.

Black Harry is introduced to us as an ex-slave who was converted in the United States of America, and migrated to the Dutch island of St Eustatius, situated between Anguilla and St Kitts.

Black Harry's heart was "full of Christ". He not only "longed its glorious matter to declare"; he resolved to "every sacred moment spend in publishing the sinners' friend".

Black Harry sought and obtained permission from Governor Rennels to preach to the slaves in St Eustatius. There is good reason to believe that the Governor and others of high standing in the tiny island went at first to audit what took place in the assembly of worship.

It was not long, however, before Governor Rennels clamped down on freedom of assembly and worship. In the then society, where the labour of slaves was a prime consideration, anything that appeared to reduce production would not be tolerated. Black Harry's style and power of preaching brought upon him the stigma of fanaticism. His listeners were not only spell bound under his preaching, but also many slaves fell to the ground as though thunderstruck, and remained "knocked out" for hours on a stretch. Such manifestations aroused alarm among the authorities. Moved by suspicion and fear of material loss, the permission, which had been given, was revoked. Local authorities shied away from "Methodist Enthusiasm".

It is not only Black Harry who was put to the test by authorities in St Eustatius! Even Dr Coke – "The Columbus of Methodism" – was required to preach privately before the Governor, when he arrived in the island in 1787.

Though satisfied with Coke's credentials and preaching, he who was "Mad About Mission" was not permitted to preach in public! The work of Black Harry was, however, already fruitful. A community of Methodist believers had been gathered. Coke remained on the island for two weeks, and further instructed and organized the flock – recognizing Black Harry as the leader.

A campaign of Suppression of Methodism and persecution of the faithful was embarked upon by Governor Rennels and his government in St Eustatius. There was promulgated what has been described as "the most egregious edict of religious persecution on record." The enactment of this law made praying in public a criminal offence.

> "If any white person should be found praying with his brethren – for the first offence he should be fined fifty pieces of eight; for the second, one hundred pieces; and for the third he should be whipped, his goods confiscated, and he should be banished from the island. If a (free) coloured man should be found praying, for the first offence he should receive thirty-nine lashes; and for the second, if free, he should be whipped and banished; but if a slave, be whipped every time".
>
> ("Pieces" the standard currency of the period).

Despite Governor Rennels' edict with its harsh penalties, Black Harry could not remain silent. He was consumed with a burning passion for souls, and bore his testimony: "Shall I the hallowed Cross to shun, refuse His righteousness to impart, by hiding it within my heart?" Ignoring the edict and continuing his religious activities, Black Harry paid the price! He was brutally flogged, imprisoned, and then banished. Mindful of the suffering and agony of his Lord, he was able to say calmly to those who jeered and hurled at him their threats: "Christ was flogged, why should not I?"

It is more than mere conjecture that Black Harry on being banished from St Eustatius returned to America. Rev George E Lawrence in his book "The Wesley of the West Indies" supports the view that the Black Harry of St Eustatius was the same as "Harry Hosier, "Black Harry", who was a favourite of both Francis Asbury and Dr Thomas Coke – pioneers of Methodism in America. Black Harry must certainly have been very effective if Oxford-educated Dr Coke could make this judgment of the vigorous but uneducated preacher:

> "Monday 29, I preached at one John Parnell's. I have now had the pleasure of hearing Harry preach several times. I sometimes give notice immediately after preaching, that in a little time Harry will preach to the blacks; but the whites always stay to hear him. Sometimes I publish him to preach at candlelight, as the Negroes can attend at that time. I believe he is one of the best Preachers in the world, there is such an amazing power attends his preaching, though he cannot read; and he is one of the humblest creatures I ever saw".

It is said that Richard Allen, founder of the African Methodist Episcopal Church, tried to teach him to read and write, but Harry gave it up when he discovered that it constricted his freedom of speech.

In spite of the violent persecution in St Eustatius, the Methodist community continued to grow. When Dr Coke returned to St Eustatius in December 1788, he found a group of some 250 persons. He baptized 140 of that number before boarding ship. The beleaguered flock was, however, surprised at the quick return of him to whom they had just bid farewell. What could the matter be? The ship's crew proved too drunk to sail the ship, and were forced to return to port! Dr Coke assumed that this was an act of providence. He therefore hired a room and preached the following day. He further announced his intention to preach again the next Sunday. Governor Rennels would have none of it, and dispatched the message: "You are forbidden to preach publicly or privately, to whites or blacks, under the penalty, in default, of arbitrary punishment". More for fear of what would happen to the flock than for his own safety, Dr Coke sailed away to St Kitts and then to fashionable Nevis where a door of opportunity was now open.

On his last visit to St Eustatius in 1790, Dr Coke found that persecution of the Methodists had waned somewhat. Notwithstanding, Governor Rennels overruled the appointment of a Local Preacher from St Kitts, and for a period of eighteen years St Eustatius disappeared from the Minutes of the British Methodist Conference.

Is it merely coincidental that the death of Governor Rennels in 1811 saw the appointment of the first missionary, Myles Coupland Dixon, to St Eustatius? He proved a "defender of the faith", and eventually was allowed by the Governor to preach without hindrance. He was succeeded by Rev Jonathan Raynar (1815–1818), and the membership moved to 320.

And so the beat went on. Methodism became and still is considered the established Protestant Church in the island. A further development of the saga is that John Seys, a nephew of Governor Rennels, outraged by the atrocities of his uncle, offered himself for service among the people who had been dehumanized by the white oppressor. As an ordained Methodist Minister, Seys served in the British Virgin Islands, in the USA and also in Liberia, West Africa.

It is men like Black Harry, and others like him, who made Methodism, confessors of which any Church would have a right to be proud, and the remembrance of their steadfastness and devotion ought to kindle anew the fire of enthusiasm within and among us today. The moral of their lives may be summed up in the stirring words on the Methodist Revival uttered by President Roosevelt some years ago:

"If we are to advance in broad humanity, in kindliness, in the spirit of brotherhood, exactly as we advance in our conquest over the hidden forces of nature, it must be by developing strength in virtue, and virtue in strength, by breeding and training men who shall be both good and strong, but gentle and valiant – men who scorn wrong doing, and who, at the same time, have both the courage and the strength to strive mightily for the right".

We therefore salute Black Harry and faithful and selfless Methodist pioneers who forged the way which not only gave birth to local Churches and congregations, but also dignity and self esteem to Caribbean people. Our pioneers knew that such inalienable human rights are in harmony with God's will for people created in His own image.

Black Harry and others like him, "have left a name behind them: that their praises might be reported." We thank God for them, even as we remember those "which have no memorial," but also served their day and generation. We who are recipients of so rich and costly a heritage, ought fervently to pray: "O God to us may grace be given to follow in their train."

Chapter 6

The Social and Economic Contribution of Methodism to the Development of Anguilla

The Reverend Cecil O A Weekes*

Life on Anguilla from its occupation by the British was organized according to the system of slavery: The Colony was administered by a representative of the Crown, supported by other employees of the Crown; members of the military for the maintenance of law and order, and for the protection of the island from invasion by foreign forces which was common in the Caribbean during those early days.

The social structure on the island consisted of the owners of the estates on the island, their paid employees, slaves who had obtained their freedom and last of all the slaves who had no status whatsoever in the society, and whose sole purpose of existence was to provide the labour on the plantations.

In his Book "Methodism And The Struggle Of The Working Class 1850–1900", Robert Wearmouth on page 141 quoted from the

* See biographical note, page 66.

Wesleyan Conference Minutes of 1891 the following statement: "though it never posed as a social reformer, yet it has gone down to the lowest strata of the community; it has penetrated the obscurest villages, it has rescued men from sin, it has created a sense of self respect; it has trained intelligence and conscience. It has led to the formation of habits of industry and sobriety. It has furnished opportunities for the exercise of skill and thrift in circumstances favourable to success. As a consequence it has changed the social ranks of myriads of Englishmen." In a very limited way, some of the sentiments could be said of Methodism on Anguilla. Its impact on the social and economic life on the island was not a head-on collision, but a glancing blow.

During the pre-abolition period, inclusive of the years of apprenticeship 1834–1838, plantation owners saw and treated their slaves as chattels. Their value was limited to their labour output and when they became incapable of supplying that labour, to be discarded as useless baggage without housing and without any source of sustenance or healthcare.

The Methodist Missionaries arrived on the scene with their evangelistic zeal and doctrinal belief that all men, irrespective of social status, whether bond or free, white or black, have eternal souls to be saved and can be saved through the preaching and teaching of Divine Truths revealed in the Bible and the response of faith in the Lord Jesus Christ as Saviour and Lord.

The Missionaries conducted religious services on the several estates on Anguilla with the permission of the Estate owners. Sunday school classes were organized for the religious instruction of the children of slaves and night classes were gradually introduced for the instruction of adults [slaves]. The curriculum consisted of reading, writing and arithmetic.

The next stage in the development in the religious and educational life of slaves and freed persons, when the permission of the Authorities was granted, was the building of churches and day schools with assistance from the Wesleyan Missionary Society in England, the collections at public Missionary meetings, donations from some sympathizers among the estate owners, and the labour of the slaves who were members of the church. Over a period of time, three churches and three schools were built: a church and school at The Valley; a church and school at The Road; and a church and school at West End, under the supervision of the resident minister. Teachers for the day schools were recruited from Methodists on the other Caribbean islands as well as from the membership of the Methodist Churches on Anguilla, until the Government of Anguilla took over responsibility for elementary education in the mid 1930's .

There can be no gainsaying the fact that the education programme of the Wesleyan Methodist Church, although very elementary and limited in scope, was a major contribution to the personal, social and economic development of Anguilla and Anguillians. However, while this programme of religious and elementary education for slaves and freed persons must not be underestimated, the years preceding emancipation, inclusive of the four years of apprenticeship, were very unusually difficult times, that called for greater visionary innovations, such as were devised and implemented in England by Wesleyan Methodism, in response to the extreme conditions of destitution among the poor working class members of the society.

The response of the Wesleyan Methodist Church to the challenge of human degradation visited upon the poor took the form of social relief programmes and economic activities such as encouraging and promoting the formation of "Friendly Societies", the Creation of a Poor [relief] Fund; the creation of Settlements/Mission Centres. Methodist class leaders and local preachers were in the forefront in the formation and running of Labour Unions, with the open approval of the Wesleyan Methodist Conference.

The Poor Fund was a substantial sum of money collected from the membership and friends of the Methodist Church, from which distribution was made on a realistic scale to the needy.

Settlements were blocks of houses either bought or constructed to provide housing for the homeless working class. Mission Centres were places where daily meals were provided free of cost, as well as clothing, medical care and other social amenities for the destitute. The first of these Settlements was sanctioned in 1889 by the Wesleyan Conference and sited at Bermondsey (a district in London). The moving spirit behind this innovative project was Dr Scott Lidgett, President of the Wesleyan Conference. He declared to the Conference "no other single force has operated so mightily as Methodism to bring us face to face with social problems . . . the spiritual movement of Methodism is the highest qualification for social work." [Wesleyan Methodist Magazine 1890 p.338].

Several such Settlement/Mission Centres were established in cities and towns, such as Manchester, Birmingham, Liverpool, Leeds, Hull, Boulton, Nottingham. [Methodism and the Struggle of the Working class 1850–1900, p.151] Some of these cities were the direct beneficiaries of slave labour on Anguilla in the sugar, and textile (cotton) industries hence should have been a source from which to seek financial aid through the Methodist Church to ease the lot of the oppressed and destitute slaves on Anguilla.

The vision, and the spontaneous response produced by the prevailing conditions of the destitute poor in England, did not prove to be exportable to Anguilla by the Wesleyan Methodist Church at a time when the Colony of Anguilla and Anguillian Methodists, and Missionaries resident on Anguilla were subjected to very similar conditions of paralyzing poverty. Had one such social programme been established on Anguilla, as in England, by the Methodist Church during those early years of emancipation, the result would have been immeasurable in terms of lives saved from death by starvation, and a powerful witness and practical 'exposition' of the Gospel of our Lord Jesus Christ. The Wesleyan Methodist Church passed up a glorious opportunity for the Kingdom of God. At that point, her vision was myopic.

The Poor [relief] Fund was indeed instituted in later years but remained a congregation based effort. It was not augmented by any initial infusion of financial assistance. Within Anguilla Methodism in this 21st century this institution is very little more than a symbolic gesture. It has not developed into anything like an effective social and economic assistance programme. However, the Poor [relief] Fund had, and still possesses, the potential for expansion into some form of social and economic co-operative programme in keeping with the spirit of the early Church demonstrated in Acts 11 in response to a prophecy concerning a severe famine that was coming on the world. In the institution of the Poor Fund, Methodism did lay another foundation for a social and economic assistance programme for indigent persons, which indeed has been taken up by the Government of Anguilla. However, Anguilla Methodism has failed to pursue the vision presented by the Institution of the Poor Fund and to develop its potential within the Church. It has remained satisfied with tokenism. The Vision of Dr Scott Lidgett as he said in his address to the Wesleyan Conference of 1890 that "the spiritual movement of Methodism is the highest qualification for social work" did not evidence itself to any great extent in an intentional social and economic programme, even up to the present time, 2003.

Glimpses of the life and conditions in the colony of Anguilla appear in correspondence from Wesleyan Missionaries to the Wesleyan Missionary Society in England pleading for assistance – sometimes for financial aid, sometimes for medicines and surgical instruments and medical books. Quite often the resident minister had to dispense medicine to, and perform minor surgical procedures on slaves in the total absence of a health care programme for slaves. The picture of the situation in the colony of Anguilla is one of extreme poverty, famine, starvation, illnesses and diseases, and no Government health care service open to the population of slaves and former slaves.

On 4 July 1832, the Rev Matthew Banks wrote to the Wesleyan Methodist Missionary Society concerning the prevailing condition on Anguilla. A few excerpts tell the sorrowful tale:

"This proverbially miserable colony is now bordering on general famine. Already many have perished from starvation and many more are rapidly pining away who have no other earthly prospect than to languish and die under the horrors of absolute destitution . . ." . . . "the contracted muscles, shrivelled skins, and despairing countenances of many of all complexion, is a most heartrending sight. Our house is beset from morning till evening with distressed objects both male and female coming to crave food for themselves or their starving children, and alas we have but little to give so that they have to return disappointed and frequently weeping bitterly, whilst others who obtained scanty relief have gone away weeping with joy and gratitude" . . . "There is not a merchant or merchant store or shop in the colony" . . . "almost compels us to stop our ears to the cries of the poor."

"The population of 3500 last census is now rapidly decreasing the only three vessels belonging to the island have been for sometime employed in transporting the inhabitants to St Thomas and Santa Cruz and many of the poor Negroes have stolen boats and absconded to other islands."

"I lately went to witness a sale of Negroes. They were brought to the door of the jail, the usual marketplace for that species of chattels. A fine coloured young woman of good character, a member of our society, and a scholar in our Sunday School was sold for $25 current, or about £4.6.8. Another woman was sold for $121/2 or £2.3.4. A man about 25 years of age sold for $21 or about £3.12.91/2. A boy was sold for $31 or about £5.7.7. Last of all an aged man of good character was sold for $6 about £1.0.0. I mention these things to show how many of our fellowmen might be redeemed from a miserable bondage on occasions like these which are of constant occurrence for a very small sum of money" . . . ". . . we had our missionary meetings in May . . . our collection was larger than at any former period. This was not expected as the general poverty is indescribable. I believe the people did what they could, and I am assured that many gave all they had."

Methodist Contribution to the Development of
Community Health Care:

In the absence of medical health care for slaves and freed people, the
burden of providing such care fell on the missionaries and resident
ministers of the Methodist Church on Anguilla. The following excerpts
from letters to the Wesleyan Mission House in England are startlingly
revealing:

On 12 January 1881, the Rev Dirk Almair Schouten, a minister
stationed on Anguilla from 1867–1909, wrote to the General
Secretaries in London. The letter was received on 26 February 1881:

> ". . . For the past 12 years I have been prescribing for and adminis-
> tering medicines to the sick in this island in all but a few cases
> gratuitously. Among cases successfully treated have been some of
> amen-or-rhea, consumption, difficult labour, epilepsy, palsy, dysen-
> tery, pro-lapse of the womb, severe fever, and hundreds of less
> serious ones. The calls on me for medicine have been increasing,
> while the increasing wants of my large family render it rather incon-
> venient to have my vials etc., replenished . . . I therefore request if
> you would send me on reasonable terms a supply of suitable medi-
> cines and one or two not very expensive but full and reliable medical
> and surgical works; if the cost is not above £3.0.0; a few dental and
> surgical instruments for simple operations . . . catheter . . . etc.
> Hitherto I have read Wesley's "Primitive Physic", and Graham's
> "Domestic Medicine", but in many cases I have felt the need for
> more information than these supply."

The Rev H B Britten wrote on 20 March 1828 to two persons: a Mrs
Parkin & Mrs Morley of 27 Hatten Gardens, London. In his correspondence, he requested they send him a medicine chest fitted out
according to a medical work entitled "A Companion to the Medicine
Chest", written by a member of the Royal College of Surgeons . . . He
asked that "the tamarinds, Glouber Salts, Magnesia, and castor oil be
left out; . . . the supply of Bark should be large, 2 or 3 lbs. or more, it
is so frequently called for and so liberally taken here".

The Methodist Mission Houses on Anguilla appeared to have served
as clinics for the slaves and the poor freed persons on the island. The
assumption can be made that here was the beginning of a very basic and
desperately needed facility that can be termed "community medicine"
albeit of a very primitive sort, (the Missionaries not being trained for
the practice of medicine). The proprietors of the Estates had access to

trained private Doctors, on Anguilla or on neighbouring islands. Here again is another important contribution to the social and economic development of Anguilla: the provision of primary healthcare to the largest segment of the population of the island.

The Unfinished Mission of Methodism in the Social and Economic development on Anguilla:

The Commission to Evangelize the nations must be expressed in a manner that recognizes the sacredness of the whole person. Human beings must not be seen simply as souls to be saved and the physical body as unimportant and, therefore, despised and abused. The concept of the Image of God after which we have been fashioned must in some way encompass the dignity of the 'flesh.' The revealed insight into the nature of man is recorded in the Book of Genesis: "Man became a living Soul", when the breath of God was breathed into his nostrils. Hence the proclamation of the Gospel must be accompanied by activities that show concern for the physical as well as the spiritual nature of humankind. This body is "the Temple of the Living God." The deeper our spirituality, the greater the constraint to become involved in ministries of caring for the whole man through social and economic programmes that uphold the Divinely endowed dignity and worth of the whole person. In doing this: "feeding the hungry, clothing the naked, healing the sick, housing the homeless" – Jesus said we are doing it to Him. May Anguilla Methodism of the 21st Century rise up to this God-given commission.

Chapter 7

The Future of Methodism in Anguilla

The Reverend Lindsay K Richardson *

The Religious Landscape in Anguilla

The Methodist Church is one of several Christian Churches in Anguilla
called upon to minister in an increasingly pluralistic society. The rise of
Rastafarianism, Hinduism, and Islam in recent years could suggest that
there is a growing tolerance for other religions, and that there is an
alternative Faith option for the residents of Anguilla.

While the failure of Methodism in the future may not spell doom for
Christianity in Anguilla – as the other Christian denominations/
Churches/Assemblies will no doubt pick up the slack; and while
Methodism is not necessarily competing against the other Christian/
Denominations/Churches/Assemblies, it cannot be denied that the quest
for the spiritual attention of the people of Anguilla will increasingly be
more challenging. Further, the challenge of holding the attention of
Methodist members will also be increased.

If we have failed in the past to hold the attention of our members,
and they drifted off to other denominations/Churches/Assemblies or

away from all Church involvement, then the future demands that, in the present, as a Church, we bring our members to a deeper understanding of the Annual Covenant relationship with our God, and require of our members a level of commitment to God and Church that is anticipated in membership.

While God has given us freedom of choice, and we are free to determine whether or not we want to be Christians and Methodist; there is no freedom of choice as to the demands of Christianity and Methodist membership on our lives. Christianity sets out quite clearly what it means to follow Christ. Methodism clearly states that members are required to be Christians. Therefore, there should be no confusion in the minds of members as to what is expected and required of them. To be a member of the Methodist Church is to be a Christian. To be a Christian is to accept Jesus Christ, not only as Saviour but as Lord – thus subjecting our will to that of our Saviour Jesus Christ. This fundamental truth of our Faith and Doctrines must be emphasized more and upheld, if as a Church we will be a force to reckon with in the Future. By "force to reckon with" I simply mean being able to stand before the community of Anguilla and declare authoritatively and convincingly, that we are the people of God.

Such commitment must be manifested in our faithfulness in worship, in service to God in the church and through the church, as well as in the community. This commitment must be marked by a life of sacrificial living that sees the call of God on our lives to follow Him as paramount.

There is no doubt that the Church of today has inherited a great heritage. The church of the future will judge us today for the part we played in preserving and building upon the heritage we received to pass on to them.

The Church today must, therefore, use its history to inform and shape its present and so ensure that the future continues to have a history that will inspire it to even greater accomplishments. When all is said and done, the success of the Church will be measured by the relevance of its ministries to the context in which it ministers.

Worship

One of the greatest challenges the Church continues to face in every age is relevancy. How relevant is its worship and ministry to the needs of the present age? The struggle will no doubt continue in every age between the younger and the older generations. This struggle to maintain the traditions and the need to adopt that which is new and popular and often more appealing to the young. This struggle is most visible in the forms of worship.

Worship, by nature, is dynamic. Worship is an experience shared by individuals grouped together in relation to their God. It is a personal yet corporate expression of love and gratitude and praise to God. The fact that it is personal opens the door for varied individual expressions of praise and thanksgiving. In that it is corporate, there is the need to hold on to that which is established and traditional. Herein lies the tension. How does the church maintain an atmosphere of worship that not only meets the need of the corporate worshipping experience, but caters to the individual wishes and desires to express oneself to God? This is a perennial question. The youth of the next 30 years will ask the same question of the youth of today who will be the "old people" of their day.

Thankfully, the Church has always responded to this challenge, even if forced to do so. Youth cannot be ignored, and while their enthusiasm for change can be taken to the extreme, their guided participation must be encouraged. As such then the Church must continue to embrace the talents and gifts of the youth of every age, utilizing them in meaningful expressions of worship. Inevitably, the youth will try to incorporate the music genre of the day, thus challenging the notion that not all music is sacred.

Contemporary expressions of dance and music are being introduced into worship by the youth. What is needed is the sharpening of these skills so that these expressions can be offered in worship in a manner that befits the atmosphere of worship. Efforts must be made then to ensure that such talented people understand the principles and fundamentals of worship which can then be woven into their choreographic and musical expressions of praise and thanksgiving. Accommodating such expressions in worship will continue to keep the church relevant to the children of each age, and signal that indeed all are welcome into the Kingdom of God. The dynamism of the church will also be seen in its ability to adopt and embrace expressions of every age.

Socio-Economic Realities

We can debate about the economy and the social realities of Anguilla, as to which is the chicken and which is the egg, but one thing is clear, they both seriously impact the other. Many will argue that the last year or two have been the worst Anguilla has seen in recent times on both the social and economic front.

Socially, there is increasing decline in the values and level of respect for authority and seniority, particularly among children and youth, and even among their parents. This decline is most visible in our schools.

Reports of gang fights, drug selling and usage, public sexual activity among students, disrespect for and attacks on teachers and their property in the Albena Lake Hodge Comprehensive School all speak to the moral decay that is festering in the wider society.

Juvenile offences are at their highest. Vicious and violent crimes have occurred signalling a threat to the 'tranquility wrapped in blue' image of our island. While such social ills, terrible as they are, do not happen everyday they, nevertheless, indicate a possible trend that, if not checked, would spell disaster for our peaceful island.

Economically, Anguilla can no longer boast of prosperous times. The global economic decline has seriously impacted our local economy, which depends largely on foreign commerce and travel. This economic slump has resulted in a shortage in available jobs, and reduced income for residents. This economic downturn is compounded by the fact that several Anguillians have accessed mortgages to sustain or enhance their standard of living. The economic situation has caused some persons to forfeit their homes, etc., while others had to seek additional employment to meet their financial needs. This striving to remain economically afloat has seriously affected our way of life as Anguillians. The strength of our society, which was the family, is now under serious threat. Increasingly, more parents are unable to be available for their children as they would love, and even grandparents are forced to seek work – granted a large number of them are much younger today. Clearly, the social cost of the economic fall out can be observed.

The Methodist Church, as it looks to the future, cannot ignore such challenges that will inevitably affect the children, youth and families it wishes to serve.

Youth Development

In discussing the topic, *"The Future of Methodism in Anguilla"*, members of the Anguilla Methodist Circuit Youth Commission raised a number of critical areas of Church life and ministry that they believe are critical to a strong Methodist future. Most of what follows germinated from this discussion.

The future of Methodism in Anguilla will, to a large extent, be determined by the efforts made and the emphasis placed on ministry to our children, and young people. It is imperative that the Church not only offer Christianity as a meaningful, beneficial way of life, but that the Church must be in a position to offer ministries that will be appealing and competitive with other alternative programmes that the community or technological world may be able to provide.

A large percentage of the current membership of the church consists of children and young people. It is, therefore, imperative that the Church recognize not only the need and the challenge of youth ministry, but the possibilities and potentiality and resources that exist in the large number of children and youth in the Church. The gifts, talents and graces that these children and youth offer to the church to be harnessed and nurtured are tremendous.

While addressing the current concerns and needs of the children and young people, the church must also ensure that any ministry being offered now to this vulnerable group equips them spiritually, emotionally, and physically for the challenges they will face as they mature and eventually take their places in the wider society.

A strong spiritual, biblical, and emotional base will be a requirement as they move through adolescence into young adulthood. They must be sufficiently supported to enable them to withstand the pull of the negative culture of the gangs, and the concomitant life styles of crime, drugs and illicit sex. The ministry to the youth in particular, must therefore, begin to address these issues more intentionally and specifically, with a view to developing a strong awareness and appreciation for the values and morals that are becoming of Christian young people.

Strong ties have to be created between the Church, the home and the School so that the lessons and principles taught are re-enforced by each institution. A ministry to young parents in particular is going to be very critical for the future. Teachers have to be intentionally brought into dialogue with parents and children with a view to fostering the kind of relationship necessary for an all round approach to saving our children and our society. The Church must play a pivotal role in this area through its Mission and Evangelism department. The working out of such a ministry could be facilitated through the Organizations and Education department of the Church, which already has a framework for the children, youth and adults to operate in. Clearly, the Church is structurally suited for such a task. All that is required now is the will, the commitment and the personnel to follow through on this vision and bring the "Kingdom of God" (*the Rule of God*) into the hearts and lives of our people. While the spiritual foundation is being set, serious efforts will have to be made to address other areas of concern.

Education

The Methodist Church in the Caribbean and the Americas has an enviable record in education throughout the region. Education has always been viewed as a vital component of the mission of the Church. No less effort must be spared as the Church looks to the future.

The prosperity era of the 1980's and 1990's has created the illusion in some of our children that education is not necessary for success in life. There have been far too many instances where children dropped out of school to engage in areas of work that generated lucrative returns – albeit legitimate work. Teachers and other civil servants laboured away to earn in a month what school drop outs earned in a week. There was no strong incentive for education.

Things have changed, and now education requirements are being attached to the menial of tasks. This has helped tremendously to create an environment where education is regarded as essential and vital to economic success. The Church must also seize this opportunity to assist in fostering a healthy and positive desire for learning.

The Church, therefore, has to consider seriously implementing after school programmes or weekend opportunities to assist students with extra classes. Such a ministry can target the children of primary school to help them get a better start in secondary school. Also, attention must be given to the children of secondary level who need extra tutoring. Again, it will be extremely important for there to be strong ties between the Church and the home so that the children will have all the support that they need. The church is blessed with several retired teachers who can offer invaluable service in such a venture. The hope is that this vision will be embraced by the church as a vital part of its mission to the community in the near future.

This education thrust must be accompanied with the availability of scholarships for the children. The Church needs to implement the necessary measures that will enable it to create a fund that will be able to offer scholarships to children attending secondary school and even assist some of those wishing to attend tertiary schools and or institutions for continuing education. The importance of such a fund cannot be overstressed given the current economic realities.

Efforts are being made to establish a National Adult Education policy that will create the framework for utilizing all the possible opportunities for continuing education for adults. The church will have a vital role to play in this area of continuing education as well.

Parenting Skills

A critical area of education and training will be that of enhancing parenting skills as part of the continuing education process. It is going to be very important that individuals are helped to recognize how integrated the various aspects of one's life are. Thus parenting skills is one of several life skills that will need to be taught given the number of teenage parents who are trying to make a fresh start in life.

Juvenile Delinquency

School drop-outs are still very much present. However, the drop-outs are no longer seeking work, because work (hard work) seems no longer fashionable. There are much quicker and easier ways to make money today without the need to get dirty and sweaty. This attitude to work sets the stage for illegal activities. Increasingly, this is the case among our youth to the extent where serious attention is now being given to the establishment of a Juvenile Centre for rehabilitating delinquents.

Education and counselling ministries are needed to assist this process of rehabilitation. Clearly some of these ministries will have to be considered on an ecumenical level, drawing on the combined resources of all the churches in the community. There are positive signs in this regard as church leaders have already begun discussions addressing this issue.

Sports

Presently, this vital activity for youth is not receiving the kind of attention it can receive from the Church. While it is true that the Church has a stated purpose and mission which is to save souls, this salvation cannot be in a vacuum. Can the Church be involved in so many areas? The answer must be a resounding, yes! While there are periodic sporting events among the congregations in the Methodist Church, extra efforts are required to take this activity to a new level. It is undeniable the role sports plays in the development of youth. The time has come for the Church to begin to examine the possibilities of inter-denominational sporting events to further strengthen the bonds within the communities and among the communities of Faith.

Employment

Several of our current children and youth will be working or seeking work to do. It is hoped that the current economic condition of Anguilla will improve to meet the increasing demand for employment by an ever bulging youth sector. In the event the economy is unable to deliver the necessary employment opportunities, the Church must be prepared to minister to these individuals. As such then, the church must be proactive now in its thinking, planning and forecasting, recognizing what the challenges of the future are likely to be, and begin to implement programmes that will enable it to assist young adults in the next ten to twenty years to be self reliant, or self employed.

Income Generating Projects

The one response to all these grandiose ideas that usually pops out is, "where is the Church going to get the money to do this?" If our history be accurately recorded in every detail, then it would be observed how often, as a Church, we have missed opportunities for mission and outreach, because we "did not have the money."

What is fundamentally wrong with this way of thinking is that it limits the value and importance of a need to the availability of resources to meet the need. This is so ironic, though understandable. It is ironic because we claim to serve a God who is "All Mighty" (El Shaddai = All Sufficient). It is understandable because we are also part of a world that places high value on balancing the budget.

We wonder why other churches are able to do so much. Close examination would inevitably reveal an appreciation of the El Shaddai nature of God, and God's ability to make a way where there seems to be none. While the Church must be prudent in its financial affairs, it must be prepared to match its Faith with Works. A spirit of boldness and courage and a willingness to follow the guidance of the Spirit of God as He reveals to us and confirms in us the ministries He wants us to tackle in His name. What should determine whether or not we do a project should not be the availability of the funds, but the urgency and necessity of the project or ministry. If the Ministry is needed or the project is critical for the mission of the Church, then no effort should be spared in pursuing it and trusting God to open doors and opportunities to fund the ministry or project.

This leads me to another area of great controversy in the Church. Should the Church get involved in business ventures? Whether or not it should, the fact remains that God has blessed the Church with resources that can be used to support the mission of the Church. Stewardship is the word used to describe this principle.

The Methodist Church of the future must be prepared to be less conservative in its thinking even as it remains prudent in its affairs. This is not a call to reckless investment or development of land and other resources, rather it is a call to recognize that we can be better stewards of the resources with which God has blessed us. This Call to Stewardship must be understood in terms of low-risk investment that would ensure that we preserve our heritage.

The one thing to be borne in mind, and the concern of most conservative thinking Methodists, is that we must keep our properties so that generations after us will benefit from them. This vital principle has prevented needless sales of property. However, the same principle has also contributed to a tendency to settle for less than what the Church could reasonably receive from the use of said properties.

The rule that the proceeds from the sale of all assets must be reinvested in other assets and be not used for recurrent expenditures etc., has also been interpreted to mean that the part-proceeds from rentals cannot be used to support the mission of the Church. This thinking is flawed in that the property is not being disposed of. It is being used to generate income. While some of the income must be reserved to maintain the project, the project cannot be seen as a mere fund raising project for the sake of fund raising, or for expanding an empire of income generating projects, but rather as an opportunity to support vital ministries that the Church is engaged in or needs to establish.

Income generating projects can be used to support our outreach ministries in education – scholarships, resource material etc., in sports, in caring for the sick and needy, in establishing new ventures – such as new congregations, and training of Ministerial and Lay staff. This is the Mission of the Church. The Church's land resources and other properties bequeathed by caring members provide us with an opportunity to be creative and prudent stewards generating needed funding for vital ministries of the Church. Such stewardship combined with our own understanding of God's requirements as it relates to tithing and free-will offerings will enable the church today and in the future to be an effective witness for Christ in every age. The question we need to ask, therefore, is not whether we have the money, but rather, "Is this what God wants us to do?" If God wants us to do it, then God – the El-Shaddai – will provide the means to accomplish it. Trust God.

Milestones

The year 2003 provides us with several opportunities for celebration, rejoicing and acknowledging the work of God in the lives of his people in Anguilla. Immanuel congregation celebrates fifty years since the dedication of its present church. Bethel congregation celebrates one hundred and twenty five years since the dedication of its present church. The Circuit also celebrates one hundred and ninety years since the start of Methodism in Anguilla. To God Be The Glory!

We can celebrate what we have inherited, but more importantly, be inspired and motivated to face the challenges of our time, confident that the same God who enabled our forebears is with us to accomplish even more if we allow Him to do so. The future, therefore, looks promising because the present provides a field ready for harvest. God is still working his purpose out as year succeeds to year. Today we acknowledge what we have received. Today we must improve what we have received and hand it on to the next generation who will, by the Grace of God, ensure a bright future for the Methodist Church and the Body of Christ.

Chapter 8

Those Who Went Forth

The Reverend John Hodge: circa 1770–1849

The Reverend John Hodge was born around 1770 and died in retirement in Anguilla around 1849. He was the first freed slave in the Caribbean to be ordained as a Methodist minister. He introduced Methodism to Anguilla in 1813. He candidated for the Methodist ministry in 1818 and was ordained in 1822. He served in the French island of St Barths, and in both Marigot and Philipsburg on the island of St Martin/St Maarten and also on Tortola in the British Virgin Islands. From reports to the Wesleyan Missionary Society in London, there is much evidence to claim that Rev Hodge was the outstanding evangelist of his day.

The Reverend C Leonard Carty, MBE: 1915–1994

The Reverend C Leonard Carty, MBE, was the first Anguillian to candidate for the Methodist Ministry in almost 120 years since The Reverend John Hodge. Leonard was born on 25 September 1915, candidated in 1938 and went to Caenwood Theological College in Jamaica as the 2nd World War broke out in 1939. He completed his studies in 1942 and was ordained in 1947. He served on several Leeward Islands District circuits, namely Antigua, St Maarten/St Martin, Montserrat, St Kitts, Tortola, his native Anguilla, and in Belize/Honduras, where he was Chairman of the District 1964–69. He served a short period in Slough, Buckinghamshire, England where many Anguillians had migrated. In 1958, he was awarded the MBE by Queen Elizabeth II. In 1963, he was Secretary of the Leeward Islands District. In 1971, he was seconded to be the Treasurer of Anguilla where he held the position until 1974. He continued his role in public service as Chairman of the Public Service Commission and Chairman of the Advisory Board of Radio Anguilla.

He married Helen Rowena Peterkin of Jamaica on 4 September 1944, and they have two sons, Leonard and David.

The Reverend Vera M Richardson, DipTh: 1918–

The Reverend Vera M Richardson was born at North Hill, Anguilla in 1918. She was educated at the Road Primary School, and gained the pupil teacher examinations, after which she taught privately for a while to pre-grammar school children. She was invited by the District Synod to candidate for the Deaconess Order, after which she attended Caenwood Theological College in Jamaica. She later studied at the Selly Oak College in England, where she gained the Diploma in Theology from London University. She was ordained as a Wesley Deaconess in February 1948 and was stationed in St John's, Antigua, after which she served for two terms in both the Jamaica and South Caribbean Districts of the Methodist Church, and one term in Guyana where she had responsibility for the Friendship Circuit for three years. She is now retired and since 1986 resides in Antigua.

The Reverend John A Gumbs: 1925–

The Reverend John A Gumbs was born in Anguilla in 1925 and attended the Valley Boys' Elementary School. After work in St Kitts and Anguilla, he was in 1945 accepted as a Lay Agent and stationed in Montserrat with The Reverend George E Lawrence. There he completed local preachers and candidates examination. He was a student at the Caenwood Theological College in Jamaica from 1947-50, and from 1950–55 he filled vacancies in Anguilla, St Martin, Antigua and Nevis. From 1955–76, he was stationed in the Netherlands Antilles. In Curacao, he was instrumental in establishing the Union of Protestant Churches (Aruba, Bonaire and Curacao), and was its first President. In 1971, he was recalled by the Methodist Church and was appointed Chairman of the Leeward Islands District, stationed in St Maarten, where he served five years and founded the Methodist Agogic Centre. In 1976, he was stationed in Dominica and founded St Andrew's High School. In 1981, he was transferred to St Kitts and in 1987 to Anguilla. He retired in Anguilla in 1990, but continued to serve for a further two years, in the absence of a minister. He is married to Veronica Gumbs nee James, and they have one daughter, Josephine.

The Reverend Franklin A Roberts, BA: 1926–

The Reverend Franklin Roberts was born in 1926. From sitting in Class at the Valley Boys' School, he assumed the role of Teacher until he left in 1945 when he was appointed a Methodist Lay Agent in the British Virgin Islands circuit. He was the youngest of '*The Holy Seven*' who entered Caenwood Theological College in 1947. Further professional training was undertaken at Selly Oak in Birmingham, England; Union Theological Seminary, New York and at the University of the West Indies. From 1950 he ministered in Nevis, St Kitts, Montserrat, Antigua, St Maarten/St Martin, The British Virgin Islands, Dominica, Curacao and in Jamaica from 1966–79. In 1985 he became Chairman of the Guyana District. He retired from the active ministry in 1990 and re-entered in 1992, finally retiring in 1996 to his homeland, Anguilla with his wife, Cassandra. His two daughters and their families reside in Jamaica and North Carolina.

The Reverend Cecil O A Weekes: 1930–

The Reverend Cecil O A Weekes was born in 1930. He completed his primary education at the Valley Boys' School in 1943. He attended the Montserrat Grammar School from 1944–50 and gained certificates in the Cambridge University Overseas examinations at the Junior, Senior and Higher School levels. He was given a "Note to Preach" while still at school, and in 1953 became an accredited local preacher. He candidated for the Methodist ministry in 1954, and attended Caenwood Theological College in Jamaica where he graduated in 1958 and was stationed at Gingerland in Nevis. He was ordained on 21 October 1960 at the Provincial Synod of the Western Area held in Antigua and was appointed Superintendent of the Nevis Circuit in 1961. From 1963–81 he served in the Jamaica District, during which time he was Superintendent of the Lucea, the Ocho Rios, the Brown's Town & Edmonson, and the May Pen Circuits. In 1981 he returned to the Leeward Islands District and was Superintendent until 1988, when he was elected Chairman of the Methodist Church in Guyana for the ensuing four years. From 1992–94 he was the Superintendent of the South Trinidad Circuit. From 1994–95 he was Superintendent of the St Kitts Circuit, and of the Antigua Circuit from 1995–96. He retired in August 1996, and in September was invited by the British Virgin Islands Circuit to reside and serve as an active supernumerary. In 1998, he returned to active work and was appointed Superintendent of the Circuit. In August 2000, having completed 48 years of active ministry and serving in four of the eight Districts of the Methodist Conference of the Caribbean and the Americas, he retired, and with his wife, resides in Anguilla.

The Reverend S Wilfred Hodge, DipTh, BD, DMin: 1932–

The Reverend S Wilfred Hodge was born on 17 January 1932. He attended the Road Primary School, and at the age of 12 years gained a scholarship to the first Anguilla High School. At 15 years, he gained a further scholarship to the Grammar School in St Kitts, where he successfully passed the Cambridge School Certificate. On graduation from high school, he taught at the Road Primary School for 6 years, 1949–55. During that time, he started the first mobile library in Anguilla, on the back of a bicycle. He has also represented Anguilla at cricket and football. He candidated for the Methodist ministry in 1955, spent a pre-collegiate year in St Maarten/St Martin before proceeding to the United Theological Seminary in Jamaica for 4 years, 1956–60. He graduated *magnum cum laude* and received the six first prizes offered by the Seminary. He also gained the Diploma in Theology from the University of London while at Seminary. He was first stationed in 1960 by the Provincial Synod to the Bahamas District and was eventually assigned to the Leeward Island District where he served in the following Circuits: Dominica, St Kitts, Nevis, St Thomas/St John, Montserrat, Antigua, St Maarten/St Martin, St Croix, Aruba and Holland. He pioneered new congregations in Nevis, St John, USVI, Montserrat, St Maarten/St Martin and Holland. He served the Leeward Islands as general secretary of Finance and Property for over 20 years. He visited England in 1967–68 on a "Visit to England Scheme" and attended Handsworth College, where he obtained the Bachelor of Divinity degree from the University of London. In 1976 he served as Missioner to the North Indiana Conference of the United Methodist Church, and studied at Wesley Theological Seminary where he obtained the Doctor of Ministry degree in 1979. He did further post doctoral studies at Emory University including a course in Theological German. In 1991, he was appointed Senior Methodist Tutor/Warden at the United Theological College in Jamaica from where he retired in 1997. He has written a number of booklets on Church-related topics. He presently serves a congregation in Anguilla, as well as Secretary of the District Resources and Development Committee. He married Jean Yvonne Campagnie in 1960. They have a foster daughter, Beverlyn.

The Reverend Joseph R Lloyd, DipMS, ThM: 1934–

The Reverend Joseph R Lloyd, was born in Anguilla in 1934 and received his early education at the Valley Boys' School. At 12 years his parents sent him to a private high school, which unfortunately did not survive for long. He returned to the Valley Boys' School where he wrote and passed the Standard Seven examination in December 1948. He became a pupil teacher in 1949 and taught for 14 years. He candidated for the Methodist Ministry in 1962 and was accepted for ministerial training by the annual District Synod which was held in St. Kitts in January 1963. In September he entered the United Theological Seminary, Jamaica for three years. He spent his final year at the United Theological College of the West Indies (UTCWI), Mona, Jamaica from which he graduated with the Diploma in Ministerial Studies in June 1967. He served in Guyana as circuit minister in the following circuits: West Demerara and Georgetown, and as superintendent in St Kitts, British Virgin Islands, St Thomas/St John, Antigua and Anguilla (Leeward Islands District). He has held the following offices: Secretary of the Guyana District Synod (1970–73); District Candidates' Secretary (LI District); General Secretary – Mission and Evangelism (LI District – 1 year); Secretary of the Leeward Islands' District Synod 1979–82; Chairman and General Superintendent of the Leeward Islands' District Synod 1982–87. Post-graduate studies were undertaken at Princeton Theological Seminary, New Jersey, USA, majoring in Pastoral Care and Counselling. He was awarded the degree of Master of Theology in May 1979. He married Joan nee Browne from Guyana. They have two children, Neville and Christine. After thirty-five years of itinerant ministry he superannuated on 31 August 2001.

Reverend Hugh Clifton Niles, DipMS, LTh, MA, MBA, ThM, DMin: 1941–

The Reverend Hugh Clifton Niles was born in 1941 on Anguilla where he received his early education at the Road Primary School graduating with a Standard Seven Certificate in 1955. He was recruited as a pupil teacher in 1956 and remained in the teaching profession for eight years. He candidated for the ministry in 1963 and entered the United Theological Seminary, Kingston, Jamaica in 1964 for two years before entering the United Theological College of the West Indies, Mona, Jamaica, where he completed his studies in May 1968 graduating with the Diploma in Ministerial Studies, and the LTh. from the University of the West Indies (UWI). He has served the Methodist Church in St

Elizabeth, Jamaica District; St Eustatius, St Thomas/St John, St Maarten/St Martin, Leeward Islands' District. Other appointments: Training and Organising Secretary for the Boys' Brigade, Eastern Caribbean Region, and sub-Regional Coordinator of The Caribbean Conference of Churches. For eleven years he was Senior Methodist Tutor and Warden at UTCWI, Connexional Conference Secretary for six years, and President of the Leeward Islands' District Conference from 1997–00. His post-graduate studies were undertaken at Eden Theological Seminary, St. Louis, Missouri; Union Theological Seminary, Richmond, Virginia; Candler School of Theology, Emory University, Atlanta, and Graduate Theological Foundation, Indiana. He married Ruth nee Richardson in 1968. They have five children – Andrew, Evona Rolle, Lauren, Elisa and Sharyn.

The Reverend Egbert Dunstan Richardson, DipMS, STM: 1941–

The Reverend Egbert Dunstan Richardson, son of Naomi and Walter A Richardson of Roaches Hill, was born in Anguilla on 19 May 1941. He was given the name 'Dunstan' because he was born on the Feast of St Dunstan, a monk who later became Archbishop of Canterbury in 960. He received his early education at the Valley Boys' School and the Valley Secondary School. At age 14 he was confirmed into membership of the Church at Ebenezer in the Valley. There he was nurtured by the Church (Sunday) School, Wesley Guild and the Boys' Brigade. He assisted as a teacher at the Church (Sunday) School at a very tender age, and subsequently assumed the office of superintendent. He came through the ranks of the Boys' Brigade (BB), eventually becoming an officer, and later Captain of the 2nd Anguilla Company. In his early teens Dunstan heard and responded to the call of God to discipleship and service. He became a local preacher and subsequently offered for 'full' time service in the Church. In 1967 he was accepted as a candidate for the ministry of the Methodist Church and entered the United Theological College of the West Indies from where he graduated with the Diploma in Ministerial Studies. He assumed his first ministerial appointment in Tobago in September 1971–74 when he was transferred to the Grenada circuit. There he served for two years before returning to his home District where he has remained. He has served in the following circuits: Montserrat, St Kitts, Aruba, Antigua, St Thomas/St John, Curacao, St Maarten/St Martin and St Croix where he is the superintendent. In addition to his pastoral duties, he has served as District Candidates' Secretary, General Secretary – Mission and Evangelism, and Secretary of the Synod for ten years. In 1982–83, he undertook post-graduate studies at Christian Theological Seminary, Indiana, USA, in Pastoral Care and Counselling, leading to a Master's Degree (STM). In 1971 he married Amy Bernadette Hodge, also from Anguilla.

The Reverend Neville Buchanan, BA, MBA, DMin: 1942–

The Reverend Neville Buchanan was born in Anguilla in 1942. He attended Road Primary School and then the Valley Secondary School, where he obtained his Cambridge Certificate. On leaving school, he went to St Kitts where he worked at the Treasury Department as a clerk. There he became a local preacher and candidated for the Methodist ministry. He began his theological education at the United Theological Seminary in Jamaica in 1965. Four years later he graduated with a BA degree and was appointed to Chateubelair, St Vincent. He was later transferred to Grenada, where he spent two years before moving to the United States to study for his doctorate in Ministry. Upon his return to the Caribbean, he was stationed in Barbados. In 1980, he emigrated to New York, where he pastored the Fenimore United Methodist Church. He is a certified counsellor, and has worked at a reform school for boys. While in New York, he completed a Masters degree in Business Administration. In 1994, he moved to Fort Lauderdale in Florida, and currently pastors a church in nearby Hollywood. He and his wife, Pat, have three daughters – Jackie, Stacey and Heather.

The Reverend Wycherley Gumbs, LTh, BA, MDiv, MEd, PhD: 1945–

The Reverend Wycherley Gumbs was born in Anguilla in 1945. He attended the Road Primary School and the Valley Secondary School. From 1963–68 he was a teacher, during which time (1967) he candidated for the ministry of the Methodist Church. In September 1968, he began his studies at the United Theological College of the West Indies at Mona, Jamaica, and graduated in 1972 with an LTh and also gained in 1973 the BA degree from the University of the West Indies. His first appointment was the Mt Fletcher Circuit in Mavis Bank, Jamaica – 1972–73. He attended Pittsburgh Theological Seminary in 1973–75 and concurrently did graduate studies at the University of Pittsburgh in 1974–75. He was the Minister in St Eustatius from 1975–78, and in Dominca from 1980–82. He returned to the University of Pittsburgh in 1980, where he gained his PhD. From 1982–88, he was stationed in Nevis. He was Chairman and General Superintendent of the Leeward

Islands District from 1988–93, during which time he also served in the St Thomas/St John Circuit in the US Virgin Islands. He is presently employed by the Government of the US Virgin Islands and is President of the Interfaith Coalition St Thomas/St John, President of the Anguilla Virgin Islands Society, and a Minister in the St Thomas/St John Circuit.

The Reverend Lindsay Keithley Richardson, BA, MTS: 1964–

The Reverend Lindsay Keithley Richardson was born in Anguilla in 1964, the second of seven children to Mr Lindsay A Richardson and Alma W Richardson of Sandy Ground. On completing High School he worked for three years before candidating for the Methodist Ministry. After four years of training in Jamaica he was appointed to serve the Jamaica District from 1989–97. After post graduate studies at Drew University in New Jersey, he returned home to serve his own people in 2000. After one year under the Superintendency of the Rev Joseph R Lloyd, he was appointed Superintendent of the Anguilla Circuit. He is married to Charmaine Rey-Richardson, daughter of the late Bernadette Pontiphlet and Hugo Rey Sr. They have one son, Charis Rey-Richardson.

The Reverend Hugo E Rey, Jr, BA, MTS: 1964–

The Reverend Hugo Rey Jr. was born in Anguilla in 1964, the son of Ms Averil Carty and Hugo Rey Sr. On completing High School, he worked for five years before candidating for the Methodist Ministry. After four years at United Theological College of the West Indies at Mona in Jamaica, where he obtained a Diploma in Ministerial Studies and a BA degree, he served in the Jamaica District from 1991–2000. After two years of graduate studies at Drew University in New Jersey, he gained his Masters degree in Theology and was granted a one year leave of absence in the USA. In 2003, he was appointed to the St Eustatius Circuit in the Leeward Islands District. He and his wife, Corlis, have one son, Hugo Rey, III.

The Reverend Jefferson C Niles, DipMS, BA: 1966–

The Reverend Jefferson C Niles was born in South Hill, Anguilla in 1966. He attended the Apostolic Faith School in St Thomas while his family resided there; and the Road Primary School when the family returned to Anguilla. He was a student at the Valley Secondary School from where he graduated with eight GCE O'Level subjects. After working at the Government Treasury for three years, he candidated for the Methodist ministry in 1987 and entered the United Theological College of the West Indies in September of that year. He graduated four years later with a Diploma in Ministerial Studies and a Bachelor of Arts (Honours) Degree. He was ordained on 31 January 1994 and has served the following Circuits in the Leeward Islands District: Nevis 1991–93, Antigua 1993–96, Dominica 1996–01 and St Thomas/St John 2001–present. He is also the General Secretary of the District's General Education Committee. He is married to Lorna Annette Hughes and they have a daughter and son, Jeffrine Anissa and Japheth Ajani.

The Reverend Erica D Carty-Lewis: 1975–

The Reverend Erica D Carty-Lewis was born in Anguilla on 18 January 1975. She attended the Road Primary School and later the Albena Lake-Hodge Comprehensive School, from which she graduated in 1991. For the next three years, she taught at the Road Primary School, after which she was attached to the Government Secretariat for a further two years. In 1996, she was the first lady from Anguilla to candidate for the ministry of the Methodist Church, and in September of that year entered the United Theological College of the West Indies at Mona in Jamaica. She graduated in 2000, and was appointed to the Kingstown Circuit in St Vincent, where she resides with her husband, Fabian, and their newborn son, Erian.

THE EDITOR

The Reverend Wilbert Forker, MBA, DMin: 1935–

The Reverend Wilbert Forker, who is the guest editor of *Born in Slavery – The story of Methodism in Anguilla and its influence in the Caribbean*, was born on St Swithin's Day in the See of St Patrick in 1935. After primary and secondary school education, he attended Shaftsbury House in Belfast and Matriculated at Trinity College, Dublin University. He candidated for the Methodist ministry in 1955 and attended Edgehill Theological College, which is affiliated to Queen's University in Belfast, Northern Ireland. He completed his studies in 1958 and began his ministry in the then British Guiana, followed by service in St Vincent and Barbados. In 1968, he was appointed Chef de Presse at the head-quarters of the World Council of Churches in Geneva, Switzerland.

From 1972 to his retirement in 2002, he was the Executive Director of the Templeton Foundation. Upon his retirement he received the Gold Medallion from the International Council of Christians and Jews for his "outstanding contribution to inter-faith understanding". From 1990 to 2000 he was a trustee of the Parliament of the World's Religions and a member of the Board of Harvard University Centre for The Study of the World's Religions. He has the postgraduate degrees MBA and DMin. He resides with his wife, Maureen, in Anguilla. They have two children, Christopher and Kathryn.

Ministers who were appointed to the Anguilla Circuit

1822	Rev John Hodge
1827	Rev Henry Britten
1830	Rev Jonathan Cadman
1830	Rev Matthew Banks
1832	Rev John Hodge (second term)
1835	Rev George Croft
1837 – 1867	(no resident minister)
1867	Rev D Almair Schouten
1910	Rev J W Acres
1911	Rev Geo. A Elliott
1914	Rev William Sunter
1916	Rev A E Belboda
1917	Rev A H Clarke
1919	Rev J A Wade
1923	Rev A E Belboda (second term)
1924	Rev A B B Baker
1934	Rev G Lawrence
1936	Rev Atherton Didier
1940	Rev L T Byron
1943	Rev A A Pattie
1944	Rev Rev E John Gazzard
1946	Rev Geo. Bedford
1949	Rev C Leonard Carty
1951	Rev Donald C Henry
1953	Rev Kenneth Derham
1954	Rev A Williams
1958	Rev D O Field
1959	Rev C E Dickson
1960	Rev J R Maddran
1962	Rev D G Mason

1965	Rev Martin C Roberts
1967	Rev Roy B L Whyte
1970	Rev Harold Gill
1972	Rev R B A Telemaque
1976	Rev Gay Nicholls
1977	Rev M Peterson Joseph
1980	Rev C Leonard Carty (second term)
1981	Rev J Evans Dodds
1985	Rev R E Brown-Whale
1988	Rev John A Gumbs
1992	Rev Neville D Brodie
1994	Rev Keith Lewis
1995	Rev T N Rolle
1997	Rev Joseph R Lloyd
2000	Rev Lindsay K Richards

Significant Dates in
West Indian Methodism

1760:   Methodism founded in Antigua

circa 1770:   John Hodge born in Anguilla

1786:   Dr Thomas Coke arrives on Christmas Day in St John's, Antigua

1813:   John Hodge founded Methodism in Anguilla

1815:   First Methodist church built in Anguilla with slave assistance

1817:   John Hodge founded Methodism in Marigot, St Martin

1822:   John Hodge ordained

1828:   The Road Church dedicated

1830:   The Valley Church was opened on 25 July

1832:   John Hodge began his second term in Anguilla

1834:   Emancipation Act passed 1 August – Slavery abolished

1840:   John Hodge retired

1883:   First West Indian Methodist Conferences (East and West) inaugurated

1903:   West Indian Methodist Conferences (East and West) dissolved

1928:   Caenwood Theological College established in Jamaica

1929:   West Indian Deaconess Order established in Jamaica

1954:   The United Theological Seminary established in Jamaica

1960:   Bi-Centenary of Methodism in the Caribbean and the Americas

1966:   The United Theological College at the Mona campus of the University of the West Indies inaugurated.

1967:   The Methodist Conference of the Caribbean and the Americas inaugurated at Belmont in Antigua

1996:   Restructuring of the Methodist Conference of the Caribbean and the Americas

1996:   Establishment of a three year Connexional Conference and District Conferences

Bibliography

ANGUILLA AND ITS METHODISM 1813-1963
by Geo F Lawrence
Privately Published in 1972

ANNALS OF ANGUILLA
1650–1923
by S B Jones 1934
Reprinted 1976 by CJL, Belfast, Northern Ireland

JOURNAL OF JOHN WESLEY
"Primitive Physic"
First Edition 1747 Republished 1986 by Lion Publications, UK

KINDLING OF THE FLAME
Methodist Bi-Centenary Celebrations in the Western Area
Published by the British Guiana District in 1960

FOR EVER BEGINNING
by Donald Ching
The story of the Methodist people in Jamaica and the West Indies
Published by the Literature Department of the Methodist Church,
    Jamaica, 1960

WEST INDIAN HISTORIES Book 1
Thomas Nelson and Sons Ltd.
First published 1936

THE CALL OF THE WEST INDIES
by Deaville Walker
Cargate Press, London, *circa* 1936

ROAD METHODIST CHURCH ANGUILLA
Diamond Jubilee 1878–1938

HISTORY OF METHODISM IN ANGUILLA
by Rev Geo E Lawrence

ROAD METHODIST CHURCH DIAMOND JUBILEE 1878–1938
Edited by Rev A Didier

CENTENARY PHILIPSBURG METHODIST CHURCH
St Maarten N.W.I. 1851–1951
by Rev R Colley Hutchinson

THE LISTENING ISLES
The Record of the Caribbean Consultation in Puerto Rico 1957
IMC London

NO HARBOUR
by Wilfred Easton
Cargate Press, London, 1959

THE METHODIST CHURCH IN ANGUILLA
150th Anniversary 1813–1963
by Geo E Lawrence & C Leonard Carty

STORY OF AMERICAN METHODISM
by Frederick A Norwood
Adingdon Press, 1974

CONCH ON THE SEASHORE
Poems of four Anguillian Poets
by CJL, Belfast, Northern Ireland, 1975

MAD ABOUT MISSION
by Cyril Davey
Marshalls, England 1985

COKE
A Bi-Centenary Publication Jamaica Methodism 1789–1989
by Rev John W Poxon

THE CHURCH IN THE SUN
by John Parker
Cargate Press, London

METHODIST MARTYRS
Lecture by William W Watty, Kingstown, St Vincent, August 1991
Privately Published

WHAT WE DO IN ANGUILLA
Official Island Guides 2002, 2003

HISTORICAL LETTERS FROM METHODIST ARCHIVES, 1819–1833
Published in London

Notes

Notes